Mirror, Mirror

Dr Linda Papadopoulos

Mirror, Mirror

DR LINDA'S BODY IMAGE REVOLUTION

HODDER

MOBIUS

Copyright © 2004 by Dr Linda Papadopoulos

First published in Great Britain in 2004 by Hodder and Stoughton
A division of Hodder Headline

The right of Dr Linda Papadopoulos to be identified as the Author
of the Work has been asserted by her in accordance with the
Copyright, Designs and Patents Act 1988

A Mobius Book

3 5 7 9 10 8 6 4

A CIP catalogue record for this title is available from the British Library

0 340 83375 0

Typeset in Sabon MT by Palimpsest Book Production Limited,
Polmont, Stirlingshire

Printed and bound by Clays Ltd, St Ives plc

Hodder Headline's policy is to use papers that are natural,
renewable and recyclable products and made from wood grown in
sustainable forests. The logging and manufacturing processes are expected
to conform to the environmental regulations of the country of origin

Hodder and Stoughton Ltd
A division of Hodder Headline
338 Euston Road
London NW1 3BH

For my adorable little Jessie

Contents

Acknowledgements   ix

Prologue   xi

1. Body Image   1

2. How We Draw Our Portrait   39

3. Food, Glorious Food   74

4. Shopping for Your Body   105

5. Your Body, Your Relationships   134

6. Your Body 9–5: Body Image and the Workplace   168

7. Plastic Surgery and Makeup: Changing the Person Looking Back   198

8. Your Mirror   226

Epilogue   249

Reference List   251

Acknowledgements

To Emma, Helen and Rowena, my editors, thank you for the support, the helpful feedback and for always being constructive when I'm sure you could have been critical.

To Jaine, one of the most beautiful women I know (even though she claims she can't see this), thank you for insisting I write this book, for fighting my corner and for being a best friend first and a fab agent second.

To Amy, for her amazing sense of humour and great writing talent, and to Sabine and Carl, thank you all for all your hard work and for sticking with the research long after you were fed up with the research!

To Trudy and Andreas, my wonderful parents. I really couldn't have done this without you. Thank you for dropping everything and being there for me whenever I needed you, thank you for giving so much so effortlessly. And thank you for giving me the foundations for a great body image. You mean the world to me.

To my wonderful little Jessica, thank you for your smiles and laughter and shouts of 'mommy!' while I was writing. Thank you for making me take breaks when I hadn't planned to and for showing me what beauty really looks like.

And finally to my partner in all things in life, my husband Teddy. Thank you for pondering the importance of commas and paragraph breaks with me, for the notes that you left on my keyboard that made my day, and for looking at me and seeing the woman I always wanted to be. I never feel more beautiful than when you look at me, you are so good for my body image . . .

Prologue

'So, what qualifies you to write about body image?' my publisher asked when I pitched the idea for this book to her.

She had caught me off guard – but then I remembered how I'd got into the whole area of body image in the first place. In 1985 my cousin developed vitiligo, a progressive skin condition that causes the appearance of white patches all over the body. Almost overnight she went from being a happy, outgoing teenager to being introverted, quiet and sad. It wasn't that the condition was that extensive or indeed that obvious, but rather that she now saw it as defining her, as making her feel less than everyone else. Thankfully, with the support of her family and her own amazing spirit, she was able to cope with the challenge of an altered appearance and now rarely gives it a second thought. But her experience in those first couple of years stayed with me, and when I was deciding on a topic for my doctoral thesis I knew I wanted to examine what my cousin had gone through.

I began to study how appearance, or more specifically our perception of the way we look, affects behaviour. I also wanted to see if I could reverse some of the negativity associated with poor body image that many people with skin conditions feel. I worked with people with vitiligo and found that many experienced embarrassment, low self-esteem, poor quality of life and very poor body image.

To address this, I developed a psychological therapy to help them cope and tested it using a series of experiments. The results were amazing. By changing people's perception of their illness and the way they viewed their bodies, they improved dramatically. Not only did their results show improvements in body image, quality of life and self-esteem, but they began to engage in activities and behaviours that they never had before. A fifty-six-year-old man, who had hated the marks on his arms and legs so much that he had not been able to wear short sleeves since he was nine, was finally able to wear what he wanted. He still writes to me, usually in late autumn, saying that the weather may be getting cooler but he's still wearing shorts and T-shirts because he just loves feeling free enough to 'wear whatever the heck I want to!' A twenty-nine-year-old dancer who had had no intimate relationships because of the negativity she felt towards her body was finally able to overcome this through therapy. In fact she invited me to her wedding last year and when I arrived I was happy to see her strolling around proudly showing off the little bump that was growing inside her.

The work I did with the vitiligo patients was published and received a lot of attention from the psychological community. In my private clinical practice I began to apply what I had learnt from the vitiligo clients with others. It appeared to work with people who had significant disfigurements and with those who just didn't like their bodies. Over the past eight years I have used the techniques I developed in that initial study with hundreds of people – and even on myself when I'm feeling low about my body image.

Which brings me to the second reason that I feel qualified to write this book. As a young woman living in a society that values beauty above anything else, I too have battled with insecurities about my body. The fact that I'm not overweight doesn't mean I'm immune to anxieties about my appearance. A lot of people think that to feel good about your body you need to be a certain size but the reality is, body satisfaction and dissatisfaction come in all shapes and sizes, so whatever your size or shape, you will not necessarily escape body insecurity. I, like countless other women, have spent a lot of money on products that promised to fix something I (or the beauty industry) had decided needed fixing. That's why I wrote this book.

The concept of body image is important in terms of how we see and value ourselves yet is rarely spoken about. When we are feeling low about our appearance we are taught to look outwards for solutions rather than inwards to the thoughts and feelings that are at the core of our problems.

By understanding and developing our body image we can liberate ourselves from the shoulds, and have-tos that prevent us reaching our full potential. Body image has the capacity to affect everything from our confidence and self-esteem to the way we relate to the people around us. Taking the time to explore it and make it work for us will give us the freedom to accept ourselves and embrace life.

I hope that by reading this book you will learn how your thoughts and beliefs about your body control your feelings about it; and that by examining where those thoughts come from, you can take control of how you feel about the way you look. This book isn't about saying that you should throw away all your makeup and go on chocolate binges because what you look like doesn't matter: it's about acknowledging that what you look like is only a part of who you are, and that minimising the essence of you to the size of your bum or the colour of your hair is as ridiculous as it would be to describe your true self as a bad accordion player. Body image is one of the most powerful concepts we have for feeling good about ourselves – and the only way to improve yours is through altering the way you think about your body, not the way you look.

I hope you will enjoy this book, and that from reading it and doing the exercises you will learn to make body image work for you.

Chapter One
BODY IMAGE

Woke up stressed about what to wear – bum still looks big in everything despite six days of low-carb dieting. Opt for tent-like black dress hoping I will be taken for quirky, Bohemian artsy type and not two-stone-overweight woman obsessed with chocolate. Before work, stop at local Starbucks – they have fruit on display but can't remember if apples are carbs or not so opt for double chocolate muffin instead. Scoff down muffin quickly in the hope that the quicker it gets down my oesophagus, the more likely it is that my fat cells won't notice it.

Get on tube and take a seat. I notice that my left thigh is hanging over borders of my seat's allocated bum cushion and edging dangerously close to that of the heavily pierced punk-type boy sitting next to me. I look around to see if anyone has noticed my unruly saddlebags (am certain everyone standing is thinking awful things about how I should be jogging to work and not taking up so much space on a train – shouldn't have eaten the damn muffin!).

Finally arrive at office where three skinny girls (probably named Trixeee, Trinee and Tilleee) are discussing travel plans for summer holidays – one cracks a joke and the others laugh – am pretty sure they are laughing – not because of their facial expression, as Botox has robbed them of the ability to do anything but stare blankly into space like bored goldfish – but I can tell by the vertical motion of their ribs clearly visible under their stretchy pastel tops.

I sit at my desk and begin to stress about the prospect of another summer where I long for ankle-length, baggy bathing-suits to come into fashion. Am awakened from daydream by very cute accounts manager, James Blazen, asking about the Strazzo account. Instead of answering I begin to imagine what he would look like in a thong and subsequently get depressed by the fact that he would never go for me because I'm not pretty or thin enough. It hurts me that he would reject me on the basis of something as superficial as looks, so when I answer I glare at him in disgust. He looks confused and walks away, mumbling.

Lunch-time rolls around and I am committed to sticking to my diet (although I have already slipped up with muffin, mocha latte and a small packet of cheese and onion crisps). Go to local sandwich bar, ask for tuna salad, no bread – hairy Italian guy flirts with me (probably because I remind him of his mother). Am now more depressed than ever.

Go back to work, look up liposuction clinics on Internet but get discouraged when I come across section that explains exactly how fat is wrenched out of one's bum and how it may return if one doesn't remain disciplined with regard to diet and exercise. Decide to look up recipe for chocolate brownies instead, and wait for five o'clock. Drag myself home, picking up a bottle of Lambrusco and an assortment of pick-and-mix on the way. Spend the rest of the evening in front of the TV with my Lambrusco, stuffing my face and wishing I was a thinner, prettier me.

Sound familiar? Well, that's probably because whether it's weight, height or frizzy hair most of us spend as much time during the day worrying about our bodies as we do about our jobs, relationships and even world events! I have to admit that even though I have researched and worked with body-image issues for years, on bad days I still catch myself thinking that I need to look a certain way to be happy. I still want to believe that the cure to cellulite resides in a plastic bottle and that wearing enough moisturiser will ensure I look twenty-five when I'm sixty. I have queued at Selfridges to buy the latest face creams, bought gym memberships I've never used and still feel weird wearing skirts because I've never liked my legs.

But I've come to realise that on good days none of this matters. I like who I am. I even like the way I look. It's not that I look different, just that I have a better perspective on things. All of sudden my legs, or hair or skin, are not at the centre of my universe. I can focus on and like *me* as an individual.

I've used this realisation a lot in my clinical practice. Whether I'm working with a client who has serious burn scarring or a woman who hates herself because she's gained weight, I know that the most important step is to help them see that the way they *think* of themselves will affect the way they *feel*, showing them that progress can only come when they realise that their perception of their bodies affects the way they feel about themselves and the way they react to the world around them.

We live in a world obsessed by beauty and glamour and a negative body image threatens our sense of identity and self-esteem. Who we are becomes inextricably linked with the way we look, and we come to reduce our identity, even our worth, to what we see in the mirror. This means that our perception of ourselves, our body image, significantly affects our thoughts, feelings, behaviour and overall quality of life. Whether it's forgoing a dinner invitation because we've recently gained weight or being late for a movie because we just can't get our hair to look right, our body image is at the core of how we relate to others and, more importantly, to ourselves.

The ideas in this book come from psychological theories and research relevant to women in real-life situations. Each chapter has a narrative running through it. The stories and characters are based on a combination of cases I have seen over the years as well as my own and my friends' experiences. As you follow the story you may recognise some of your own hopes and fears in the characters of the narrative. I hope you giggle with their experiences but also that you are touched by them too – this may help you to gain insight into your own feelings and thoughts about body image.

The first two chapters focus on the theory behind body image, uncovering the reasons why we see ourselves as we do. The first chapter is an overview of the key concepts I'll be discussing in the book, including a description of the building blocks of body image and self-esteem. The second deals specifically with how body image develops through life and, in particular, how our experiences affect the way we view ourselves. The middle chapters deal with body image in relation to specific areas of life, including relationships, sex, work, dieting and shopping. The final chapter draws together all the ideas that the book puts forward and discusses how you can maintain the progress you will have made by reading it.

Each chapter ends with a *Take Away* – a series of psychological exercises to help you put into practice the book's key messages. They are based on psychological research and have been adapted to address the most common problem areas relating to body image. Make sure that you spend the time and do these exercises properly, to really benefit from them.

Our view of the world is, to a great extent, dictated by how we see our position in it: if we feel confident and secure our worldview is more positive than if we feel bad about ourselves. The perception we have of ourselves and our bodies is subjective, affected by everything from our mood to the situation we find ourselves in. But just think about it, if you could change your perspective, perhaps those things you don't like about your life will change too. If beauty is in the eye of the beholder then you, as the beholder, have the capacity to define how you see and value yourself . . . so sit back and enjoy the journey to a more healthy, powerful, positive view of you . . .

What is Body Image?

If you ask women to describe how they look, or what they think of their appearance, most churn out a list of negative phrases: 'too fat', 'too skinny', 'too spotty', 'too short'. They aren't necessarily accurate – in fact, they may be totally wrong – but they summarise how they see themselves. For instance, imagine waking up one morning to find that you've developed the world's biggest spot on your nose. You feel its presence every waking moment, it's like another entity, a horrible little monster attaching itself to your face and following you around. You cake it in tea tree oil and cover up, knowing that in five minutes it will rear its ugly head again. But everyone else? Well, they can't even see it. Body image isn't based on fact, it's not a tangible concept – it's based on a group of thoughts and feelings we have about ourselves.

Psychologists define body image as 'a person's thoughts, perceptions and feelings about their body'. This means that what we see in the mirror is not our actual appearance as judged by others but, rather, our subjective judgement about how we look. '

We start to create our body image as soon as we become aware of ourselves as individuals at around the age of eighteen months. This is when children recognise themselves in a mirror, and when the word 'I' enters their vocabulary. This new awareness of ourselves will serve as the foundation of our body image. Body image is an abstract concept, what psychologists call a *mental representation*. Mental representations are important because they allow us to make sense of our world, and we have them about everything we see and experience – from what a dog is to what love means. The way we interact with the world depends on this knowledge.

There can be a vast difference between the way we see ourselves and the way others see us. Our view of ourselves doesn't only depend on what we see in the mirror because it isn't only our eyes that construct our perception. What you see when you look in the mirror is affected by everything from your mood at the time to things your mother said to you in childhood. For instance, if before you look in the mirror you (a) have a flashback of your mother telling you how pretty your brown eyes are; (b) have walked past a group of men (preferably not working on a building site) who stared at you in awe; or (c) have had another woman ask where you get your hair done, you will see a very different you from the one you may encounter if (a) you recall your mother saying, 'Honey, you're not wearing your hair like that, are you? It makes your eyes look even smaller than they really are'; (b) the workmen on a building site ignored you as you walked by; or (c) you were advised by an old woman with a blue rinse on how to deal with split ends.

There is no such thing as just looking in the mirror:

the judgements of others, illness, disability, the way we were brought up, the family we were born into all play a part in painting the picture we see when we look into the mirror.

Different cultures place different emphasis on the size or shape the body should be. Think big bottoms in Latin America, or small feet in China. In eighteenth-century China we might have asked 'Do my feet look big in this?' as easily as 'Does my bum look big in this?' in twenty-first century Britain. Poorer cultures see thinness as a sign of poverty, malnutrition or illness while plumpness is a sign of prosperity and health; in wealthier cultures we associate health and prosperity with slimness, and being overweight with laziness and unhealthiness.

There is great variation in the way different cultures value skin colour too: in certain parts of Asia pale skin is valued to the point that women use hydroquinone, a potentially harmful chemical, to lighten their skin; in the West, women bask in harmful UV rays to get the deep golden-brown skin indicative of beauty in our culture.

In some cultures, especially those where women hold the economic power, the stringent prescriptive indicators of beauty are placed on men instead of women. In the Nigerian Wodaabe tribe, men compete in beauty contests judged by women and spend hours on their makeup and clothes to make themselves attractive to females.

Culture plays a huge role in shaping the values by which we live, no matter how ludicrous. Next time you pick up a copy of *National Geographic* and are staring with amazement at the tribes who stretch their bottom lips or elongate their necks with rings, think of how all our face-painting, stiletto-wearing, fat-sucking and boob-implanting practices look to them! Even more importantly, ask yourself why such practices seem so natural to us.

Not only does culture play a significant role but other experiences such as sexual or racial harassment may also impact on our body image. In our culture today certain racial features are valued above others, therefore your cultural identity and its impact on your life will inevitably be relevant to your body image. This is particularly significant as so many of us live amongst cultures and communities that are different from the ones that we were born into. If you are an African European child growing up in a predominantly white neighbourhood, where all your friends, neighbours and toys look different from you then your body ideals and, consequently, your body image will be affected. Likewise, if you work in an office where your breasts get as much attention as your memos you are bound to develop a body image that has at its core the way your breasts look! You see, our body image is not something we are born with, like eye colour, or skin tone, it is something we acquire through interaction with our environment and others. Knowingly or not, we revisit it several times a day. Whether it's flicking through a magazine, gawping at Jennifer Lopez's bottom, or agonising for hours in front of the full-length mirror that *must* be lying to us, our body image is a backdrop to all our thoughts, feelings and behaviour.

Liking What's on the Inside

Our self-esteem is integral to our body image. If you don't like yourself as a person, it's unlikely that you will like your body, and surprise surprise, if you don't like your body, chances are, you won't be crazy about yourself as a person. Like body image, self-esteem is determined by the judgements a person makes and maintains about themselves. Unlike body image, self-esteem doesn't relate specifically to appearance but is broader, and includes intelligence, physical mastery, emotionality – in fact, anything that has the potential to make us feel adequate or inadequate.

Self-esteem is not static or one-dimensional. We actually divide it into categories, which allows us to feel more positive about certain aspects of our lives. For example, 'It doesn't matter that I'm too unattractive and overweight to be in a relationship, at least I'm the best damn accountant this office has ever seen!' See where the problem lies? By doing this we highlight and reinforce those parts of our lives where our self-esteem is low. To increase it, we need to work on it as a global concept, not give up on certain parts. It's true that at times we feel more or less confident about different aspects of our lives and situations, but general self-esteem is more vulnerable to change than each individual section. Even if you are convinced that your accountancy skills are better than anyone else's, unless you work on your self-concept as a whole you will never achieve high self-esteem.

In many ways, self-esteem is about believing in yourself – in your abilities and seeing yourself as worthy of happiness. It is linked to what we feel we deserve. This is an important idea, since many of us believe that meeting our own needs should come second to meeting the needs of others. The fact of the matter is that until you can believe that you are worth making time, worth making the effort, and worth taking risks for, then your self-esteem is not going to shift.

The Relationship Between Body Image and Self-esteem

How do body image and self-esteem work together to convince you that because you have gained four pounds over Christmas life isn't worth living and that the only meaningful relationship you will ever have is with something made of chocolate?

Self-esteem, like body image, is affected by the fact that we always see what we expect to see. If, for example, we walk into a boutique and expect the assistant to treat us rudely because we don't feel glamorous enough to be there, we will focus only on those behaviours we perceive as being rude or try to explain away any ambiguous behaviour as rude because that is what our expectations dictate.

Self-esteem affects our general perception of life, and our perception of ourselves. If you already have low self-esteem and a consistently negative body image, your self-esteem has to battle that negativity to grow. It works the other way round too: people who have high self-esteem have more positive expectations about their interactions with others and then consequently a more positive self-esteem and body image.

Simply stated, having bad body image can lower our self-esteem. Some psychologists have suggested that up to 33 per cent of our self-esteem is directly related to body image. Which means that the way we value ourselves is linked to how we think we look. And if one is negative, it's likely that the other will be too. Equally, a healthy body image usually equates to a high level of self-esteem. Body image is concerned with the way we see ourselves, self-esteem with the way we feel about ourselves, based on judgements we make according to many factors, one of which is body image. As one improves, undoubtedly the other will too.

By now it should be apparent that your thoughts play an integral part in your body image. People with poor body image tend to spend so much time and allocate so much of their attention to hating their bodies that eventually they separate them from their identity. Now, this may seem far-fetched, but when you think about it it makes sense: if you are experiencing a deep rejection of yourself because of the way you look, the reality is that it's easier to concentrate that self-loathing on a specific part of your body rather than hating the whole you. This kind of *depersonalisation* is often present in weight-related self-consciousness, when people identify themselves with their face rather than their whole body. The reasoning behind this seems to be 'I hate my body, but my face I can live with.' Unfortunately, by doing this, what that person is doing is underscoring the negativity they feel about themselves by rejecting their own body. Eventually, the worry they feel about not being the ideal weight or looking the ideal way is just a smokescreen that serves to hide the self-loathing that they actually feel.

The way we make sense of what is happening to us, what we feel, dictates how we behave. If we don't feel confident about our bodies or, indeed, ourselves as a whole, we often look to other people to provide reassurance and validation. We might be prepared to endure ridiculous diets and painful surgery to attract the attention and affection of others. For example, someone who feels lonely may attribute this to being 'fat', and assume that the route to finding companionship or love is to lose weight. Someone who hates their nose may blame it for all their problems, so consequently, they reason that the key to changing their life must be a nose job. We make such links and assumptions all the time, fixating on one body part and making it the scapegoat for every problem we face. Or assuming that if we can just gain control over our weight/skin/chest size, then everything will automatically fall into place, and we will gain control over everything in our life. Many psychologists believe that eating disorders are what happens when people making an attempt to become more attractive and/or gain control go too far.

Someone who has a good level of self-esteem, respect for and the confidence to stand up for themselves and what they believe in can be described as having reached 'autonomy' – literally 'living according to one's own laws'. Unachieved autonomy, which means living in accordance with everyone else's expectations and desires, is not only a feature of body image and eating disorders but also of the preoccupation that so many of us have with food and our bodies. More and more, psychologists are realising exactly how essential a healthy body image is in gaining this autonomy. There is now strong evidence to suggest that wealth, power and popularity are not as crucial to happiness as previously thought. According to current thought, we need self-assertiveness to be happy, with the ability to feel in control of our fortune, competency and, most of all, a strong sense of self-esteem.

By now it should be clear that the way we perceive things affects the way we feel about things, so looking in the mirror can give you insight not just about how you look but about how you feel as well.

The Way You See You

*O*K, I can do this . . . just take a deep breath and think calming thoughts, right? I made it, I'm here, I am in the girls' changing room, surrounded by three full-length mirrors and six down-lighters. What sick, disturbed, sadistic mind came up with the idea of putting down-lighters in a changing room? If they accentuate every dimple on my face I can't bear to think what my bum is going to look like! I mean, isn't the whole point that they're trying to sell you clothes, not make you feel like running off and attaching yourself to an industrial-sized fat-sucking vacuum! And why's the stupid curtain that is meant to act as a door too narrow to cover up the entrance? I keep catching that annoying elf-like salesgirl who looks about twelve looking at me! I know she's dying to come up to me for the third time since I've been here and say, 'Are you sure you don't need a bigger size?'

Right. I'm going to do this. I mean, if I can't face myself in a bikini then there's no chance that anyone else will be able to. I'll just focus on my face while I slip my jeans off . . . My lord, the pores on my nose are HUGE! (Mental note to self: must remember to get more apricot scrub.) OK, jeans off, bikini bottom on, am now looking at toes . . . Not bad, although second toe from right has remnants of last month's pink nail varnish. (Mental note to self: must remember to buy more nail vanish remover.) Moving up to ankles, on the plump side but still pretty shapely – but a lot hairier than they looked in the shower this morning. (Mental note to self: must buy leg wax.) Right! Knees – I am starting to feel weak, the cellulite has actually travelled to my knees! My legs look like two huge uncooked doner kebabs. (Mental note to self: buy every cellulite cream on market and book appointment with GP to discuss anti-depressant medication.) Well, things can't possibly get worse – in for a penny in for a pound (or several stone, in my case) – I will look at my bum . . . OH, MY GOD!

Bum was certainly not this big last summer – my cheeks seem to be oozing out of the bikini bottom like the Swiss cheese on my mother's broccoli soufflé. How can something grow so much so fast? OK. Don't panic! Have brought in matching sarong because I knew something like this would happen. OK, sarong-look isn't working, just makes me look like I'm hiding something, like I've wrapped my soufflé in a large layer of puff pastry. (Mental note to self: never, ever eat cheese again.) I have at this point lost the will to live let alone shop, but some masochistic part of me urges me to try on the bikini top. I put it on and open my eyes. As I try to suck in my flabby belly it becomes painfully obvious that if I intend to breathe on the beach my belly will protrude, considerably. I lift my arms to make my breasts look like they are perkier than they are only to notice that where I used to have triceps I have a jiggly piece of meat which I'm sure I have heard referred to as a chicken fillet.

Throw my clothes back on and leave the changing room feeling depressed and defeated. I hand over the evil bikini to the twelve-year-old elf, and as I walk out I hear her say, 'We're expecting a shipment of larger one-pieces next week. Pop in!' (Mental note to self: breathe deeply, do not punch elf.)

If you were asked to draw a self-portrait, parts of it would be very different from the reality – perhaps the thighs would be a bit wider, or there'd be more spots or wrinkles. The closer your portrait resembled reality (allowing for those with less than Van Gogh-like talents) the better. What you see when you look in the mirror isn't just a reflection of how you look on the outside but a combination of your physical self, your thoughts and feelings. On a good day tousled hair is sexy, on a bad day it's messy. The thing is, though, that to 'see' and 'accept' yourself as you are, you have to learn not only to see yourself accurately, but be able to separate the negativity you may feel about other aspects of your life from the way that you look. By doing this you will learn to like what you see, and feel positive about it. More importantly you will learn to question why you don't like certain parts of your appearance and decide to what extent this dislike is based on the way you think about things rather than what is reflected in the mirror.

The more positive you feel about yourself, the more likely it is that you will behave confidently and react more positively to those around you. It's like a self-fulfilling prophecy: you expect people to react positively to you, so they do. A better body image filters through to most aspects of our life, it suggests underlying confidence and emotional stability, which result in a higher degree of self-esteem. Everything, from going to the beach to going on job interviews, becomes easier – simply because we like who we are.

Now and Then

If you've decided that you don't like the way you look, this decision probably didn't occur to you overnight, it's more likely something that has developed over a long time, starting when you were a child. Whether it was realising that the good princess in the fairytale was always beautiful or that your favourite pop stars were always pretty and petite, you got the message as a child that you should look a certain way to have a good life. Although many things work together over the course of our lives to contribute to the way we see ourselves, two of the most powerful factors involved in the way we process information about our appearance are past experiences and our current understanding of what's happening around us. Let's start with the past. The way we process information about our looks can be affected by knowledge that is already stored in our memory, which may influence the way we categorise and understand incoming information. So, our perception of anything starts with an idea we already have stored in our minds. Any self-assessment can only be made within the framework of an already established self-concept. It's like when you meet somebody who you have heard a lot about for the first time.

If you have heard that this person is very annoying, that they talk too much and lack personal hygiene skills, you form a picture of them based on that information. When you actually meet them for the first time it's very hard to build an opinion of them outside this preconceived idea. In fact, what happens is that you expect not to like them, or, even, you expect them to reject you so you reject them first. It's the same with body image, the reason we constantly confirm a negative body image is because it is difficult to break free from perceiving ourselves as we have done before. Even if what we see in the mirror isn't so bad, if we have a negative, preconceived notion of what we are looking at, then we won't like it no matter what.

Now, even though past experiences can programme us to view our bodies negatively, it doesn't mean we're doomed to a life of hating how we look. The one thing that is more important than the way we interpret experiences from the past is how we interpret experiences from the present. Depending on how you choose to make sense of things in the here and now, you will either reinforce your negative body image and feel worse about yourself or you will begin to reject the negative thoughts that make you feel bad about yourself and gain a better body image.

It's amazing how one little remark can send you flying to the stars or plummeting to earth. But, as any cognitive behavioural therapist will tell you, our perception of what goes on in our lives dictates how we feel and react; first, we evaluate a situation, and then we respond to it emotionally. For example, imagine that you are having dinner with your boyfriend and starting to tuck in to Ben and Jerry's newest variety of ice-cream: he leans over and says, 'Are you going to eat all of that?' You might interpret this as:

(a) This ice-cream is so yummy that I want to eat the rest of yours, too, so please can I lick your bowl, and maybe that little piece of chocolate from the corner of your mouth, you cutie!

Or:

(b) You fat disgusting pig, I thought you were on a diet and instead you've piled your bowl so high with ice-cream that I can barely make out your third chin behind it, not to mention that your farm-animal-like table manners mean that you have a chunk of chocolate hanging on for dear life at the corner of your mouth – you disgust me!

Spot the difference? You will hear what you expect to hear, and if you aren't careful, your reaction to what you *think* you heard might have no connection to reality.

At the core of being able to gain a more realistic perspective in the present, a perspective that isn't tainted with the negative beliefs and expectations from the past, is learning to identify negative thoughts. Once you can identify irrational or negative thinking patterns you will be able to gain a clearer perspective on all your life experiences, especially those relating to body image. So let's see if you can begin to spot some of the most common *thinking errors* that most of us – at some point or another – have been guilty of.

THINKING ERRORS

All or nothing thinking: refers to thinking in extremes – either 'I'm a size eight' or 'I'm a huge Ms Blobby-like being that needs her own area code.'

(By doing this what you're doing is seeing the world in extremes, in black and white. We all know that to make sense of anything, we need to accept that we live in a world shaded by grey! Otherwise nothing we do, say or look like will ever seem good enough.)

Maximising the negatives: attending to only the negative aspects of appearance so that the way you look becomes the defining feature of who you are. 'It doesn't matter that my skin is looking better, that I feel more fit and I won the lottery, I still feel awful because my ankles are skinny.'

(In maximising the negatives you will only ever focus on things you don't like about yourself, which means that the things that could potentially make you feel positive about yourself go unnoticed.)

Personalising everything: feeling responsible or upset about things that have nothing to do with you, and trying to relate to yourself everything that happens. 'He didn't sit next to me on the bus because my skin is so awful.'

(By personalising everything you miss out on other – often significant – things that are happening around you and may help you evaluate and react rationally to what you're experiencing.)

Jumping to conclusions: reaching conclusions based on insufficient or inadequate evidence. 'It may seem that they're laughing at a joke but they're really laughing at the way I look in this mini-skirt.'

(In all likelihood you can't read minds, so jumping to conclusions will only upset you and lead to a self-fulfilling prophecy

where your behaviour brings about the negative reaction you expect.)

Seeing everything as a catastrophe: thinking of only the worst-case scenario and exaggerating what might happen. 'I've gone up two dress sizes since last summer. That means the seat-belt on the plane won't fit and I'll need an extension. They might even need to move people to redistribute the weight in the plane because of me! How embarrassing! Everyone's going to stare and laugh. That's it! I'm not going.'

(Here, you're at risk of denying yourself enjoyable experiences, not to mention becoming over-anxious about things that should be a relatively neutral part of your life.)

Generalising the negatives: exaggerating the effect of an unpleasant experience so that it affects other parts of your life, no matter how unrelated. 'My last boyfriend said that he didn't like blondes, which probably means most guys don't, which means I'll never have another relationship.'

(You are allowing negative or irrational thoughts in one part of your life to contaminate other parts, thus making negativity a bigger part of what you experience.)

So, what we think (consciously or not) is the reason for what we feel and, consequently, do. Negative or irrational thoughts lead us to behave in a way that will probably bring about a negative response from our environment and cause us to feel bad. The only way to address the think-feel pattern is to spot thinking errors, then replace them with more constructive rational alternatives. Next time you catch yourself in a downward spiral of negative thoughts about your body, stop and think about how grounded in reality those thoughts really are. Consider the possibility of a more rational, positive alternative.

Judgements

Body image is often determined by the judgements we make about ourselves. These can be approving, 'I love my hair', 'My legs look great in this skirt', or disapproving, 'I have too many freckles', 'My nose is too big.' They relate directly to our own feelings of competency and self-worth. If you feel awful, you'll judge yourself as looking awful. If you feel inadequate as a person, you may feel physically inadequate. How often when we feel uncomfortable or insecure do we doubt or criticise the way we look? All the time.

No matter what body image you have constructed in your mind, it's more than likely that one thing has had the impact of a sledgehammer on your judgement: the judgement of others. You know the feeling when you've bought a new outfit that initially you weren't sure you could carry off? You thought your legs were too short or your boobs too small? But you've come round to the idea, persuaded yourself you can get away with it. You take a deep breath and step out, feeling confident and attractive. You feel great, not only because you look great but because you've overcome a fear. All it takes is one withering look or nasty comment, and you want to run home and burn the thing. Why? Because we tend to see ourselves the way we believe others see us.

So, worse than seeing ourselves in our own mirror, we see ourselves in a mirror that *someone else* is holding up to us. Other people's judgements become just as important, if not more so, than our own. Yet assumptions we make about the way other people see us are often hugely inaccurate. Research shows that when people are asked how their friends see them they tend to overestimate the consistency of the judgements: generally they assume that everyone will say the same thing about them – and they're wrong. Although most people can anticipate the general evaluation, they can't predict differences between individual judgements. In reality, our image of others' impression of us is just a projection of our own body image on to them. In other words, we think people see us just as we see ourselves.

Yardsticks

*F*ollowing the bikini shopping trip and the severe depression that ensued (causing a major chocolate-eating relapse), I was desperate to focus on something else so when a memo arrived on my desk with thick black letters that read 'It's that time of year again: the office spring ball!' I was relieved. I picked up the sheet of A4 and pondered whether to go or not. The downside, I thought to myself, was that everyone would be there, having made a mega-effort to look good; the upside was the free wine (and thus, 2–3 hours into the evening we'd all look like Baywatch babes anyway). Nevertheless, I found myself hyperventilating every time I thought about it. I couldn't stop stressing about what to wear and how I'd look – especially compared to all the other women that show up at these things. I mean, even our photocopier mechanic Martha (formerly known as Marcus) looked better than I did last year.

After six phone calls to my girlfriends and three glasses of wine I decide to go. I meet my friend Trudy at the entrance of the tacky 4-star hotel and try to dodge the helium balloons, that are obviously trying to escape, as we enter the ballroom. I look around and my eyes fall on a large girl in a sparkly pink dress and I pray (yes, I honest to goodness say a prayer) that I don't look as big as her. I grab Trudy's arm – she shrieks in pain – I let go, apologise quickly, and make her swear to tell me the truth: am I bigger than the sparkly pink girl or not? Trudy is taking an evening course in psychology. Instead of saying something to the effect of 'Of course not, you're not even half her size, you sexy minx,' like a proper friend, she comes up with 'You're acting ridiculous and I'm not engaging with you on this matter.' At this point I'm ready to either A: Thump Trudy, or B: Remind her that she's not Dr Phil; but then I notice the sparkly pink girl getting up to dance with James Blazen (a.k.a. cutest guy at firm whom I've had a crush on for months). I can't believe she's actually up there on stage, confidently jiggling around, flicking her hair with her chubby little arms and mouthing the words to 'Come on Eileen', while James is gently patting down his hair and doing what I think is his version of the moonwalk around her. At this point (because I'm not deep enough into a parallel universe already) Trudy leans over and says, 'Doesn't she look sexy tonight? Wonder where she got that dress from?' I nod, attempt a smile and walk towards the bar, hoping that alcohol will make things a little clearer.

As I sip cheap wine from a cheap glass, I hear a chirpy little voice behind me: 'Anyone sitting here?' I turn around to see the large sparkly pink girl, sweat running down her forehead and chubby cheeks flushed and glowing. I mumble no, so she sits next to me and proceeds to down two glasses of wine, then delicately starts sipping a third. 'Hi, I'm Suzy! Why the long face?' she asks. 'These things are always so much fun!'

'Really, you think so?' I say.

'Well ya, with guys like James around – let's just say he brings out the tiger in me!'

I refrain from making a Kellogg's Frosties joke, excuse myself and go to the ladies' loo where I stand in front of a water-flecked mirror and stare at myself, wondering how I measure up in sparkly pink girl's book . . .

We've all done it, walked into a room and looked around to see how we measure up to everyone else. The way we feel in a social situation (whether we're there by choice or not) affects our self-esteem. We evaluate our self-worth by comparing ourselves to other people with whom we have things in common. For example, a mother might compare herself to the others waiting at the school gates, a sixteen-year-old girl will probably compare herself to others at school, and a track runner might compare herself to the others in her athletics team.

Perhaps this is why communal changing rooms pose such a massive threat to so many women. Not only is there the fear of other women's judgement – the paranoia that they will be looking at your tiny boobs with disgust. This is compounded by the fact that your self-esteem will take a battering as you compare your boobs to everyone else's, and such is the nature of inaccurate body image, you will probably come to the conclusion that yours are the 'worst'. Our self-esteem is not a complete, absolute evaluation we make ourselves, but one that is subject to social comparison. Many of the judgements we make are made entirely in the context of comparison.

Yardsticks exist because we are conditioned to buy into certain cultural falsehoods about life. They influence our expectations and the way we lead our lives. This is especially true with regard to women's relationships with their bodies and with other women. For example, we are led to believe:

Falsehood 1. It is possible to be objectively, universally beautiful; if you are beautiful, your life will be wonderful and all good things will come to you.

Falsehood 2. All women want to be beautiful more than anything else in the world – and so they should: it is the most important thing they can be.

Falsehood 3. Men only want beautiful women: they will fight for them, kill for them, do anything in their power to possess them.

None of these is true. There is no such thing as 'objective' beauty: rather, as we've seen, it's determined by politics and culture. Feminist writers assert that if women's value is assessed by physical standards, they are forced to compete unnaturally between themselves for resources that men have, such as power and money. It is this competition that makes yardsticks central to the way in which we relate to each other: every woman around us becomes our rival in vying for the resources we are after, until our relationships are no longer characterised by sisterhood and friendship but by competition. John Berger famously said, 'Men look at women. Women watch themselves being looked at. This determines not only the relations of men to women, but the relations of women to themselves.' It captures the way we feel about ourselves *and* the way we feel about each other.

Who Sets the Body Standards?

Who decides that big noses are attractive or unattractive, and whether it is more desirable to be petite, like Kylie Minogue, or tall, like Eva Herzegova? These values are established by the societies we live in and the people we are surrounded by. Our beliefs on body image are constructed in the same way as any other group of values we learn to accept as true. For example, our society teaches us that recreational drugs are bad, education is good and theft is wrong; we accept these values almost without question. In the same way we accept the values that dictate standards of beauty.

At the end of the nineteenth century, women accepted that the ideal was a plump body and pale skin. This body was longed for as it represented wealth, the means to enjoy sumptuous food and a refined, indoor lifestyle. Women went to great lengths to ensure they stayed out of the sun, to avoid getting a dreaded freckle, or, horror of horrors, a tan. Today a tan represents wealth, it suggests the means to take exotic foreign holidays. Despite the health risks we now associate with sun-worship, it's hard to imagine reverting to the skin-tone values of a hundred years ago. Can you imagine everyone crowding under umbrellas on the beach or *Baywatch* episodes with acres of white flesh? It just goes to show how fragile and fleeting body-image ideals are.

The ideal body has changed with each period. In the early 1900s the corseted, hour-glass look was in vogue. If you weren't the 'perfect' shape naturally, then you were bound, pulled, tightened and throttled until you were. Imagine bust, waist and hip measurements that would make Barbie look in proportion. Think back to those period dramas or history books with pictures of aristocratic ladies bent over dressing-tables while maids hoist the laces of their corsets to the point of suffocation. Think heaving bosoms, chins resting on cleavage and pencil-thin waists. Now you've got the idea.

In the 1920s women wanted to look like boys. Curves were out, slim hips and flat chests were in. In the fifties and sixties voluptuous breasts and hips were back. Who can forget Marilyn Monroe's curvy figure, barely encased in that flimsy white dress, as she stood above a strategically placed air vent? Hair was big, lips were big, eyelashes were big, hips were big and so were breasts. The look was feminine and sexy.

Since then, we have been exposed to a body-image ideal that is at best unlikely and at worst unattainable. Women with exceptional figures have been marketed as 'normal'. This body image is not only unrealistic, it is also unhealthy. Much has been made of Barbie's powerful impact. If a woman existed with Barbie's proportions, she wouldn't be able to stand up and her organs wouldn't function. And Barbie is often one of the first images of a female body that we hand to our daughters. But surely she can't be responsible for every body image problem – after all she's a busy lady, she's got a husband, ponies and a Malibu beach house to run.

No, Barbie is just one tiny aspect of the group of cultural norms we feel pressurised to live up to. The advertising industry plays a huge part in constructing and attempting to enforce these norms. Some psychologists have suggested that an image of a woman in a newspaper advertisement has the potential to destroy another woman's health, her sense of well-being, to break her pride, and undermine her ability to accept herself as a woman. Others say that it is not the complete image of the woman that does the damage, but the focus on one particular part of a model's body – lips to sell lipstick, legs to sell tights, breasts to sell . . . well, everything. This is in contrast to the way that the male body is generally shown in its entirety, and it encourages women to reject or accept individual parts of their body, rather than seeing themselves as a whole person and leads to 'I hate my bum/legs/earlobes [delete as applicable]'. We allow ourselves to obsess over one body part because it interferes with our fulfilment of the Western ideal of overall perfection.

Body image is not only about how we look, but about the assumptions we make of people's personalities, judged purely on their appearance. In some ways obesity has become a social liability, influencing people's values and lifestyles. Whether you attract a contemptuous look when you order sugar with your coffee or you have to go to special shops to buy clothes in any size bigger than a sixteen (even though it's estimated that 47 per cent of British women wear a size sixteen or above), overweight people are consistently made to feel inadequate in our society. Literally and metaphorically, they are made to feel that they don't 'fit in'. Perhaps it's because obesity symbolises lack of will-power or self-control in a society that admires self-control almost above all else. The shame we feel when we move up a dress size isn't because of the fat *per se* but the stress associated with the shame and with the discrimination we attract for being overweight. Many equate a thin, toned, 'perfect' body with self-discipline and emotional strength. Studies have found that fat symbolises inferiority and worthlessness in today's society. In whose interest is it to encourage these associations? Well, dieting is a multi-million-pound industry . . .

How Does Body Image Differ Between Men and Women?

Woman: *Does my bum look big in this?*
Man: *Does my crotch look big enough in this?*

Woman: *I love a guy with a sense of humour.*
Man: *A bald head is no laughing matter.*

Woman: *Barbie is an unrealistic, unattainable image to live up to.*
Man: *I could take GI Joe any day!*

Woman: *I hope he can't see my cellulite when we make love.*
Man: *God, I hope I last long enough to get through all that fore-play she's expecting.*

Men have always seemed to have a different take on their bodies from women. Don't they always seem slightly proud of the little paunchy belly, just resting over their trousers, that most women would be horrified at? Or alternatively, they're the ones who could have fast food intravenously fed into their bodies twenty-four hours a day and would still be stick thin. But in recent years this has changed; men seem more and more concerned about their appearance. Previously, women were scrutinised, lusted after or rejected. Now, as they become aware of media-promoted ideals of the male body, men find themselves on the other side of the fence. Phrases like 'six-pack' now refer to their body image, not what they drink on a Friday night. This has been called the 'Brad Pitt Syndrome', and television role models, pop stars and even Action Man toys have been accused of contributing to it. Just as many women yearn for long legs and a tiny waist, many men want a lean, muscular frame, with a rippling, washboard stomach and bulging biceps. As the size of male genitalia is discussed in endless 'Does size matter?' women's magazine articles, men are becoming increasingly conscious of how they fill out their underwear, too. And just as it has taken a while for men to become as concerned about their appearance as women, it will undoubtedly be a while before society recognises that body-image disorders can affect men too.

Because of this lack of discussion of male body disorders, many men often fail to realise that they may be suffering from a body-image disorder. In fact men and boys are often reluctant to reveal how they feel about their bodies because they are embarrassed or ashamed, and they typically do not recognise that their beliefs about their appearance are inaccurate. New terms, like 'muscle dysmorphia', have been coined to describe the irrational feelings of inadequacy that lead men to take anabolic steroids. This can take on obsessive, addictive proportions and because men are less inclined to talk about their condition, through shame, it is harder for doctors to spot.

So, just as Barbie has been charged with encouraging unrealistic expectations in women, can GI Joe and Action Man be accused of doing the same to men? Well, it seems that these lumps of plastic have a lot to answer for. Over the last thirty years, the male dolls have become more and more muscular, their proportions completely unrealistic. Many modern action dolls are a lot beefier and more muscular than the largest human bodybuilders, and that's without the use of steroids (unless Action Man has a few little skeletons lurking in his plastic cupboard). It's not surprising therefore that, unlike women, men's dissatisfaction with their bodies is not just about being slim: they are equally likely to want to be heavier too. The ideal body shape for a man is the muscular V, which is associated with Western values of masculinity such as strength and power. Interestingly, when men decide to change their body shape they are more likely to use exercise than diet: their way of correcting what they see as wrong is by *doing* something rather than *denying* themselves.

Until recently even the scientific community ignored men's bodies: the majority of body-image research focused on women. Stereotypically, society associates physical concerns with women. Boys are often seen as oblivious to body ideals. Yet they become aware of differences in body shape at about five years old; there is evidence that boys as young as eight are concerned about their weight and want to be slim. The difference is that girls are encouraged to talk about these worries, while boys are less inclined to do so, perhaps in the fear of being seen as less masculine. Next time you ask your partner whether he thinks your bum looks big in this, spare a moment to reassure him about the way he looks: he may not seem insecure about it, but that doesn't mean he isn't.

However susceptible men are to body-image disorders, women are still way ahead of the game. Research has shown that they are more likely to be affected by such problems, and when they are, they are likely to be affected more seriously. Perhaps it's because society teaches women from an early age that their value lies in their attractiveness and sexuality. This means that we learn young to see ourselves as objects for visual inspection and development – like a car. We put all our efforts into making sure we're a Ferrari rather than a Robin Reliant. Consequently, this may mean that women start to lack confidence in competency-based social activities, which don't call on them to look great. How does this start? It has been suggested that teen advertising and other media are partly to blame: they focus more on self-beautification, with articles on 'How to make that cutie yours with six shades of eye-shadow and a lip-gloss' type articles rather than features promoting identity development.

An important difference between men and women in relation to body image is that men look at bodies in an entirely different way from women. A man will look in the mirror, assess his image as a whole and say, 'Yep, I look fine.' He probably won't say, 'Well, on the whole I look OK, but my arms could do with a bit of toning, and perhaps my skin could be clearer.' When women look at their bodies they divide them into pieces and judge each individually. You see, through the power of advertising and marketing, we have been taught to see our body in sections. So we assess our arms, legs, boobs, face etc. separately. It's much healthier to look at ourselves as a whole, and realise that although our 'whatevers' don't look like the ads, they fit with our overall shape, which we *are* happy with.

Obviously it benefits these companies and their advertisers if we are unhappy with the way we look because they're waiting in the wings with a cream or lotion that will defy gravity or turn back the clock. An entire industry is based on the fact that when we become insecure about a certain aspect of our body we will do anything to fix it – anything, of course, that involves nipping out to the chemist rather than examining where the insecurity is coming from.

Women especially have a lot to overcome in terms of the current beauty media climate. We are made to measure ourselves against ideals of physical perfection and eternal youth, even though it's impossible for 99 per cent of women to look like the sixteen-year-old Brazilian models that adorn the pages of our favourite glossy magazines. This inevitably forces us to live in a climate of constant disappointment and rejection of our bodies. Here are some interesting facts:

- 90 per cent of all girls aged three to eleven have a Barbie doll, an early role model with a figure that is physically and medically unattainable in real life.

- A study of one of the most popular magazines for adolescents revealed that in the majority of issues the largest percentage of pages was devoted to articles about appearance (Schlenker, Caron, Halteman, 1998).
- 69 per cent of female television characters are thin; only 5 per cent are overweight (Silverstein, Peterson, Perdue & Kelly, 1986).
- The average person sees between 400 and 600 ads *per day* – that is 40–50 million by the time s/he is sixty. One of every eleven commercials contains a direct message about beauty (not to mention indirect messages).
- Exposure to idealised images lowers people's satisfaction with their own attractiveness.
- Women compare themselves to images of other women even when they aren't asked to do so (Posavac, Posavac & Posavac, 1998).

About Face: Facts on the Media, Liz Dittrich.

Now, having said all that, I really think that it's too easy to blame glossy magazines and TV for all our body-image woes. Most of us know about the magic of airbrushing, lighting and makeup – I mean, when we buy a cheeseburger at a fast-food restaurant it never really looks like the picture on the menu but we are happy to accept that, because we never really expected it to. But when we see a picture of a model who has been made-up, styled, photographed and airbrushed by some of the best in the business, somehow we want to believe that the image is real and that consequently we should look like that when we wake up in the morning or after an eight-hour day at the office!

Yes, sex sells. Yes, there is too much pressure to live up to an impossible ideal. Yes, the majority of models don't look like the majority of real women. So we need to become more proactive in not buying what is shoved down our throats.

We need to start to feel that our identity isn't only bound up in the size or shape of our bodies, we need to develop a deeper, more holistic sense of who we are so next time we look at a magazine we can see the pictures for what they are: pictures – arbitrary ideals imposed on us by the media and a fashion industry that know insecurity sells. Look at the styled, lit, retouched photos, ignore the Nazi-like beauty articles, giggle at the articles on twelve-hour orgasms, note down the must-have handbags and shoes of the season and then use the rest of the pages to line your hamster's cage with, because, you see, it's wallpaper, cheap decoration – it is not a manual for living your life or learning to love yourself.

Does Beauty Ever Feel
Like the Beast?

So what about those really beautiful women? Surely they can't possibly have any anxieties about their bodies. Surely no one believes a supermodel who says, 'I hate my thighs,' or 'It's all lighting!' Well, there is evidence to suggest that beautiful women are more likely than others to feel self-conscious, as they experience more of the evaluative gazing discussed earlier.

Of course, some personality traits influence how a woman sees herself regardless of beauty. Neuroticism often goes hand in hand with worry, anxiety and emotional sensitivity. Neurotic people are more likely to self-objectify. Perfectionism also comes into play: women who set themselves high standards and are goal-directed are more likely to conform to social expectations, less likely to discuss body insecurities and more likely to suffer from eating disorders. Even those women who seem to possess superpowers are as likely, if not more so than the rest of us, to have the same insecurities.

However, in some ways beautiful women do have it easier. It has been found that physically attractive people are offered assistance more readily, find jobs more easily and have more influence on others than less attractive people. Also, physically attractive people are generally judged in a more positive light and are automatically attributed with qualities such as sociability, good character and mental health. Many theorists have concluded that more attractive women become less focused on their appearance. Let's face it, we all have one friend who's just effortlessly beautiful – she'll just 'throw' on a scruffy, old T-shirt and look amazing when the rest of us, in the scruffy, old T-shirt, would just look, well, scruffy and old. However, despite what we may suspect, beautiful women, as well as men, have worries about their bodies too, it's just that they feel less comfortable talking about them. But for every man who wants to be more muscly/less hairy/better endowed, there are ten women who want to be less fat/less skinny/have longer legs or smaller breasts.

But why? What stops us accepting our lot? And why can some women do this and others not?

Well, simply stated, it's about perspective. As we go through life, we feel differently about our body. We go from being completely unaware of it as a baby, to it becoming the axis our universe pivots on at puberty, and then find ourselves completely bewildered by it as we go through illness, pregnancy, and eventually the menopause and ageing. You see, no matter what we do in life, where we go, who we meet, there's one thing you can bank on: your body's coming with you. And it's just as well really. Imagine if you had a friend who shared all these experiences with you, who was there 24/7. Imagine if they had to put up with the torrent of abuse many women direct at their bodies. Imagine if you attempted to change, mould and 'perfect' them, because you simply weren't happy with them. It's just as well that our bodies don't have the ability to up and leave, because, when you look at it this way, most probably would.

Developing a healthy body image is about seeing what is there *accurately*. And once you've seen your own mirror image truthfully, it's about accepting what you see. And letting it become the key to your self-esteem and confidence, rather than a hindrance. If Snow White's stepmother had had any sense, she'd have smashed that meddling mirror straight away. If she had worked on her own body image, she would never have had to ask, 'Mirror, mirror, on the wall, who's the fairest of them all?' She wouldn't have needed its reassurance . . .

TAKE AWAYS

The first step towards looking in that mirror and liking what you see is understanding how the way you *think* about things affects the way you *feel* about things. This chapter showed how our beliefs affect our perception of ourselves. Learn to identify the negative or irrational beliefs that are holding you back. Then it will be only a matter of time before you can change them.

So, let's get down to business. Begin Task 1. Don't worry if you find it strange at first, it gets easier the more you practise. Make sure that you take the time to think about the outcome of each task, focusing always on how your thoughts affect your feelings and how your feelings affect the things you do.

TASK 1

Over the next two weeks keep a diary (use Table 1.2 and see 1.1 for an example) of every negative or anxiety-provoking thought you have about the way you look or what you eat and the situation that triggered it. Fill in only the first three columns.

At the end of each week make time to look over your diary and see if you can spot any of the thinking errors discussed on page 18.

Look at the last two columns and ask yourself if you can re-evaluate your thoughts about the events you noted down. Once you've done this, note whether your feelings about those events have changed.

TABLE 1.1 (Example)

Actual or anticipated situation	Negative automatic thoughts	Emotion/behaviour	Alternative rational thoughts	Emotion/behaviour
Joining new gym	*Everyone is going to look at how big I am – I won't fit in. I'm going to fail*	*Anxious, upset, wanting to hurl gym bag out of window*	*People at the gym will be focusing on their own bodies much more than they will on mine. Going to the gym is about doing something for myself, not about pleasing other people. I can only fail if I give up*	*More positive, less anxious. Have decided against act of violence on gym bag*

TABLE 1.2

Actual or anticipated situation	Negative automatic thoughts	Emotion/ behaviour	Alternative rational thoughts	Emotion/ behaviour

See how it works? When you can spot and change negative thoughts you will have a clearer, more positive outlook and feel better about yourself. Continue with the diary for the next few weeks. You'll soon see a difference in the way you think. Once you've got the hang of it move on to Task 2, where you will look at yourself through somebody else's eyes.

TASK 2

- Make a list of five things you love about your appearance. At least two of the things on your list need to be above the neck and at least two should be below the neck.
- Now ask your partner and / or best friend to do the same for you.
- Spend some time talking about the list. How does it make you feel? What are your automatic thoughts about the other person's list? Do you agree with them? Believe them?
- Look in the mirror again with the other person's list in your hand. Focus on the body parts they mentioned. How do you feel about them now?
- Write your list again.
- Has it changed? Why? Or why not?

The point of this task is to allow you to start changing the way that you see yourself. By focusing on the positive aspects of your appearance you will begin breaking out of the negative cycle of just seeing things that you don't like about yourself. Also by asking others to tell you what they see when they look at you, you'll have to acknowledge the fact that there are other ways of looking at yourself.

Chapter Two

HOW WE DRAW OUR PORTRAIT

*C*ontrary to my better judgement and every self-preservation instinct in my body, on Thursday night I agreed to let my sister drag me to the Mate in Heaven dating agency. She assured me that three of her office friends had met 'the right type of man' through it, and that as I wasn't getting any younger (I am three years older than Lucinda but she and the rest of my family act like I'm a spinster out of some 1940s movie) I really ought to try it.

I arrived at Knightsbridge tube station where she was waiting for me. She looked immaculate as always and I noticed that she had taken to giving me the once-over the way my mother does when she sees me. She greeted me with a pitying yet warm smile, and said it was a shame I hadn't had a chance to make an effort with my outfit. She then pulled a thread from the lapel of my coat and (I swear this is true) licked her finger and tried to wipe away the smudged mascara from my right eye! I held back the urge to slap her and told her that if she didn't stop treating me like I was her five-year-old daughter, I would leave. She ignored me and motioned excitedly for me to follow her into a converted Victorian house.

While on the outside the stately residence had an aura of class and elegance, the inside looked like a cross between an American cheer-leading convention and the Barbie section at Hamley's – everything in there was so pink and sanitised it made me want to vomit (but strangely in a very ladylike, neat way). We were immediately greeted by Amelia, who seemed very excited with life generally; she rushed over to give me a hug and introduced herself as my 'love coach'. Amelia had a blonde bob and a long fringe that came just above her sparkly blue eyes. She wore a mauve business suit and had a heart-shaped pin over her left breast that read 'There is someone for everyone, even you . . .' She sat down opposite me and began to reel off the pre-written and pre-memorised company mission statement.

Apparently, in order to 'actualise the dream of meeting my soul-mate' I needed to learn to sell myself – in a non-prostitute sort of way of course, she hastened to add. She explained that I had to make a video message describing myself that they could show to potential partners. Now this, it seemed, was extremely important and my words needed to be crafted 'just so' if I was going to manage to snare Mr Right, because, as Amelia put it, 'A man doesn't want a frowny-faced party-pooper who doesn't like herself! He wants a sexy, ladylike honey bunny who loves, loves, loves herself! When you look into the camera don't think of the size of your thighs, think of the size of your heart!' she cooed. Just for the record, after Amelia's pep talk I vowed never to speak to my sister again, let alone take dating advice from her, but before I could make my excuses and sprint out the door Amelia had ushered me into another pastel room where a pouffy chair stood ominously across from a camera. She handed me a remote control and some instructions, and told me I had thirty minutes to complete my three-minute tape.

Now, to a lot of people, describing themselves might seem like an easy enough task. I mean, you start with your hair colour – which you can easily get details of from the box the dye came in, lie about your height, weight and hobbies and, Bob's your uncle, you've done it. But for me, i.e. someone who spends most of her life avoiding mirrors and trying not to draw attention to herself, this is a very daunting task. As I sat in my uncomfortable pouffy chair, I began to think about how I really saw myself. Don't get me wrong, I think I'm generally OK, a *good friend and a great Pictionary team-mate, but when it comes to how I look . . . well, I just hate even thinking about it.*

As I stared into the camera I remembered comments made by others about me: 'Pretty face, but big-boned like her aunt Cecilia'; 'Has her dad's nose but with the right eye makeup you won't really notice it'; 'Not really a ballerina's build but very flexible for her size'. It occurred to me that every statement I could remember about myself was in some way negative. I realised that over the years the image I had built up of myself was so bad that I was actually dreading having to talk about me. I willed myself to think of the positives, as Amelia had advised; unfortunately all I could come up with were things like 'My nail varnish is a nice colour' and 'Lino gave me a good haircut this month.'

After twenty minutes of sitting there depressed and defeated, I managed to look into the camera and say, 'Twenty-two years old, five foot nine, blonde, huge boobs, a tiny waist and golden skin, love football, beer and dolphins. If you're interested then – piss off! cause men like you and women like that make me sick.'

I walked out, handed the tape to Amelia and marched down the road towards the chocolate section in Harrods food hall.

What we see when we look in the mirror is a portrait of ourselves, not a complete portrait, mind you, but a work in progress that we add to and edit throughout our lives. During some periods of our development we put a lot of effort into developing this portrait (a.k.a. our body image), while at others, especially in the earliest part of our life, we are to a great extent completely oblivious to the way we look. Babies are not concerned about body image. That's a fact. And you don't need to have studied child psychology to know that. Next time you see a baby, just look at its bottom; now imagine a grown woman wearing a big, bulky babygro. It would never happen. Ever. Because babies are not concerned about body image, and the majority of grown women are. So how do we get from being blissfully unaware of the size of that enemy hanging just below our spines, to living in a world where our bottom is our master?

The fact of the matter is that we need to be aware of ourselves and how others respond to us early on in order to manipulate our environment. As babies, we discover that by smiling at an adult we can make him or her do more or less anything we want – and so we begin to form beliefs about how we can affect the world. We use this knowledge to make sense of our world, and we develop beliefs about how things work, sort of global truths or core beliefs that help us to understand our experiences. These core beliefs determine how we interpret reality, how we make sense of our world and how we see ourselves fitting into the world around us. They serve as maps that influence what we pay attention to and what we filter out. Our core beliefs become so much a part of who we are that we don't even know they're there, we take them for granted and live our lives by them, rarely stopping to question them.

It is from these core beliefs that any negative or irrational thoughts about more specific areas of our lives develop. Core beliefs are bigger, broader and more global than negative thoughts, which tend to be more specific and detailed. A core belief that says you must be appealing and pleasing to others to be accepted by them can lead to negative or irrational thoughts, such as 'I must lose weight before I start dating again,' or 'No one will like me the way I look now.' Negative thoughts can be about our relationship with food, clothes, beauty products – anything to do with appearance.

They relate to the core beliefs you hold about how your appearance affects your life. The problem is that if we develop unhelpful core beliefs the negative thinking that derives from them will become so routine that not only will we find it difficult to stop them, we won't even recognise we're having them. This leads to feelings of inadequacy and despair about the way we look.

As we saw in chapter 1, our body image develops from our past experiences and the way we see ourselves in the present. This makes it difficult for us to establish between a past and present 'me'. Differences between the two are merged into a continuous identity, adding to the inaccuracy of the way we see ourselves. This is especially true of negative comments we have heard about ourselves. Memories of past experiences can cloud our judgement. Think about it, how many of us hold on to negative feelings about a school nickname, even though we have changed since then? If we were known as Spotty, our skin will be the thing we focus on, Beanpole, our weight, Shorty, our height . . . you get the picture. If your past has taught you that a certain part of you is not good enough, then that's the first thing you're likely to focus on when you look in the mirror.

Our core beliefs act as the raw materials we use to paint our portrait – the canvas, the brushes, the paint. If they are dysfunctional, they will lead to negative thoughts and irrational interpretations about our experiences. No matter how hard we try, we will never be able to develop a portrait that does us justice. That's why it's imperative that we take the time to understand, first, where our core beliefs have evolved from; and, second, how they affect the way we interpret what goes on around us in the present.

Childhood

Like most things that come to haunt us in adult life, the formation of our core beliefs starts in childhood. Initially, children construct their view of the world in a very different way to adults. As they grow, they develop increasingly complex core beliefs. Obviously, as they gain more experience they have more information to base their core beliefs on. As children have new experiences that conform to an existing core belief, they take them on board. And when they come across situations that do not fit in with the existing core belief, children adapt the core belief to incorporate the new information. If you hold a toy in front of a baby, she will reach out and grasp it. Then she will study it, first visually, then by putting it into her mouth. She will use the experience to add to or modify an existing core belief. This process also applies to core beliefs about the child's self-perception.

From birth until they are about two, babies gain knowledge of the world through their senses and movement (as opposed to gaining knowledge by thumbing through encyclopaedias). This is when they first begin to identify their bodies as separate from Mummy's or Daddy's or the dog's. They are aware of their bodies at this stage, but they do not judge or assess them. At this age, babies also begin to understand that their gestures and actions are mirrored by their parents. For example, when you see an adult staring into a pushchair, chanting, 'La-la-la', or 'Coochi-coochi-coo', they probably haven't lost their minds, they're just mirroring the noises of the little one. Mirroring increases the child's understanding of social relationships, and as soon as they begin to recognise that their parents' actions reflect their own, they start to build up a better picture of themselves.

This early understanding of how our parents see us is integral to the development of how we see ourselves. Imagine that a baby is hungry and begins to cry. If the parents respond immediately with concern, mirroring the baby's distress and making them feel contained and safe, they will grow up with the core belief that the world is generally a safe place, that people are basically good and that they are lovable and worthy of care and kindness. If the baby's cries continually go unheard, or when a parent responds they don't mirror the baby's distress and respond effectively the baby learns that the world isn't such a safe place, that they can't rely on people to meet their needs and that they aren't lovable or worthy of care.

Now as well as seeing our image reflected in our parents, babies are also fascinated by the mirror as they begin to understand its function. However, even as early as fourteen months they may shy away from it. Unbelievably, between the ages of fourteen and twenty-four months, children may demonstrate the age-old fear of the mirror. Until this point, the mother has acted as a 'mirror' to the child, and reacted to their every movement. Around this age, the child becomes aware that they exist as a separate entity to Mummy, they realise that the mirror *isn't* Mummy.

Self-consciousness may arise through embarrassment over genitalia. At this age, children are investigating their bodies, and while a deposit in the potty may be praised, playing with 'private' parts at the dinner table is unlikely to elicit the same response. Children begin to realise that experiencing and experimenting with genitalia is frowned upon, in some contexts at least, and this can also cause them to become self-conscious when naked and confronted with a mirror. They begin to get a taste of the concept of negative feelings towards one's body (but let's be honest, they don't know the half of it).

Childhood experiences are integral to how you see yourself today. To see how this applies to you think back to an early childhood memory that evokes strong emotions in you. Try to remember the first time you were aware of feeling uncomfortable or embarrassed. Perhaps you were watching your mother put on her makeup and hearing her complain about how awful she looked, or an older sibling laughed at your freckles, or you came into a room in your new Sleeping Beauty pyjamas and didn't get the attention and praise from Daddy that you expected. Any of these experiences may have contributed to how you see yourself today. The makeup experience could have come to underscore the belief that looks are very important and something valid to be upset about; the freckle teasing might be a reason to feel different or 'less than' your siblings or peers, and the Sleeping Beauty pyjamas experience gave you an indication that other people may not share the positive view that you have of yourself. The point is that childhood experiences, even though they may seem insignificant on the surface, are often the origin of the negative core beliefs that we carry around with us throughout our lives.

The Wonder Years: Adolescence

Adolescence. It's one of those profound life-changing processes that we all go through and is scarier and more confusing than *The Exorcist* and quadratic equations rolled into one. As we enter it, our body is changing faster than at any other stage we can remember. We're caught on a roller-coaster that we can't stop or get off. No matter what teenagers do, hips will grow, breasts will appear, hair will sprout and just in case that isn't scary enough, spots will top it all off. Adolescence is a time when body-image concern in young men and women is at its peak: all those physical changes, the soul-searching and identity-building mean that the first thing you think about when you wake up and the last thing you think about before you fall asleep is the way you look.

More than anything, this is a time when we examine ourselves in relation to others, and our self-image is particularly challenged when we meet new people whom we like or feel are important, and begin to measure ourselves against them. Since we develop at different rates from our peers, we try desperately to get a grip on what is 'normal', and whether we fulfil that criterion.

At this time in our lives the people whose judgements we care about most are our friends. Our feelings about our own rate of change depend largely on them. It's OK to be the second or third girl in a group of friends to begin periods or grow breasts, but the first? Terrifying! Or the last? Even worse. However, early pubertal development in boys is actually admired and respected, which is great for the first to discover a pubic hair and develop a deeper voice but not so good for little Billy who still sounds like a choirboy at fifteen. Adolescents find it difficult to challenge cultural stereotypes of femininity and masculinity as they are still learning what it means to be a man or woman in society. No surprise, then, that they resort to anything, from piercing their noses and dyeing their hair to smearing their skin with countless potions, to control their bodies. In fact for some young people, disorders such as anorexia nervosa and bulimia develop as a way to grasp some control over their rapidly changing bodies. It is estimated that the onset of puberty brings with it a 20–30 per cent increase in body fat. By now, of course, girls have already established that society deems fat undesirable, so this increase can be embarrassing, distressing and confusing.

As quickly as the physical changes of puberty occur, the core beliefs we have formed about our appearance and self-worth update themselves. For example, if a thirteen-year-old walks into school and is called Pizza-face, because of acne, she will reassess the way she looks at herself. Others see her differently and, more importantly, negatively, prompting thoughts like 'If my skin was clearer, more people would like me and life would be better.' She may go on to 'I hate my face' – and an array of negative thoughts and self-hate ideas. In ten years' time her spots may have disappeared, but the feelings of inadequacy will prevail. Whenever she feels down, or gains weight, or has a blemish, the same inadequacy core belief, the old fears and anxiety will tumble into her mind. We often assume that when we leave the playground we will move on, but an insecurity created there may stay with us for life. For many people, once a Pizza-face or 'the fat girl', they will always feel, deep down, like Pizza-face or a fat girl. Old core beliefs die hard.

And it's not just our peers throwing around nicknames who impact upon how we see ourselves. In fact, just as when we were babies and young children, our family's behaviour may have a profound effect on how our core beliefs develop. Whether it was your mother's pleas to do something about the bushy eyebrows you inherited from your father's side of the family or the way that your father always seemed to favour your sister because she was the prettiest (no matter how hard he tried not to show it), we get messages loud and clear from our families about the expectations they have of us and the way we look. Of course, it's not just our parents: often we pick up on the way that our siblings act too, so if we've grown up with an older sister who is constantly on a diet, we learn that thin is good, fat is bad, and that food has a lot more power in our life than we previously thought. This message is then incorporated into our core beliefs and we carry it along with us for the rest of our lives, or until we become aware of it and learn to challenge it.

Although we begin to form our core beliefs as young children, as we enter puberty our experiences may reinforce or challenge them. The messages we receive from the people around us throughout childhood and adolescence can have a lasting effect on our body image. As we've seen, adolescence is a time when the need for approval from our peers is paramount as it will dictate our position on the social ladder and affect our prospects of dating. Unfortunately, such approval isn't always forthcoming. Most of us can probably remember being teased about some aspect of our appearance while we were growing up. But while some of us are affected significantly by this, others go through life with a perfectly healthy self-portrait. Why?

Research has consistently shown that people with high self-esteem fare better in dealing with knockbacks relating to their body image – in fact, they cope better with most things in life – than those whose self-esteem is low. Self-esteem is the best defence against the shoulds and have-tos that we grow up with, and those who feel valued, competent and loved are less likely to fall into the trap of believing that self-fulfilment results from perfect looks.

We have established that our body image is often irrational, and so is the sense of perspective we place on different features. We look at a tiny pimple on our forehead as if through a magnifying-glass; we imagine that when others look at us, they are fighting to hide their disgust. In reality no one notices it. Yet when someone compliments us on our great teeth or fantastic body, we can't even see it. 'No!' we protest. 'Really I look awful today!' or 'No, seriously, if you could see me naked – I'm so fat! It's hideous!' In adolescence, the magnifying-glass creeps in frequently. As teenage girls establish that the ideal body is slim and toned, their hips expand at a rate of knots. As they start to long for the flat stomach of a fashion model, a little tummy bulge appears. Well, 'little' in reality – in the mind of that girl, she looks about seventeen months pregnant. Body image, at any age, is not about reality or actual measurements, it's more like a hall of magic mirrors, where nothing is as it seems.

The Age of Consent

Ah . . . first dates! They seem like such a lovely romantic idea in principle but rarely do you escape feeling anything but confused and deflated. By our late teens or early twenties most of us have started dating, but, unfortunately, with the excitement of the first kiss comes the possibility of humiliating rejection. Yet again, we are reminded of how important our appearance is in order for us to be accepted and date, and pair up, just like everyone else. But despite the alarming rate of physical development, social skills, such as diplomacy and tact, are often left far behind. All it takes is one cruel knockback for us to form or rekindle damaging core beliefs. And this, of course, can happen throughout our adult lives.

Negative beliefs about who we are have the potential to become so powerful and so dysfunctional that we begin to dislike not only how we look but who we are. The depth of the self-hate we can develop because we feel inadequate in some way is astounding. To hurl abuse at yourself becomes commonplace, even comfortable. According to Aron Beck, the father of cognitive therapy, the interesting thing is that the hatred we hold for ourselves develops in much the same way as the hatred we may develop for others.

Here's how it works: if someone offends us, we look first for some flaw in them to explain their actions – for example, insensitivity, tactlessness or selfishness. Then we generalise this negative trait, and turn it into a summary of their personality: 'He's a spiteful person.' Once we have made this judgement, we may retaliate to hurt them in return. Finally, we may decide to end the unsuccessful relationship. The same analogy works with body image: when we decide that part of our appearance is bringing us un-happiness, first we criticise it: 'I hate my tiny breasts.' Then we generalise: 'I'm so unattractive.' Finally, this can lead to self-hate, and then self-rejection: 'I hate myself'; 'I'm worthless.' We try to disregard our body, just as we would the person who upset us. This explains why looking in the mirror then becomes so hard.

Throughout life self-hatred, or dissatisfaction with our bodies, means that we adopt stringent criteria for what we deem acceptable in how we look. This is because we feel that by being harshly critical we will buffer ourselves from the negative reactions of others – especially potential part-ners. The thinking process behind this is: 'If I'm as hard on myself as possible I'll be prepared for any reaction from someone else, no matter how negative.' We may begin to do some 'all or nothing thinking' (as discussed in chapter 1) i.e. 'Because I don't have the figure of an underwear model, I must be a short, dumpy lump no one would ever want to go out with.' We tell ourselves that if we are not one extreme then we must be the other: 'If I don't have a perfect tiny nose I must be lugging around an elephant's trunk on my face.' You may tell yourself, 'If only I was taller, he'd go out with me.' Or worse still, 'There is no way anyone could find someone as tall as me attractive, so there's no point in trying.' To 'protect' yourself, you put up a barrier that keeps people out so that you can never be hurt or rejected. If a guy smiles at you in a bar, you shoot him down with a dismissive glance: if you reject *him* first, he won't have a chance to reject *you*. If someone asks you out on a date, you assume they're teasing you, and it's part of a big joke, so you knock them back with a sarcastic put-down. And so the 'solution' in dealing with the poten-tial rejection becomes part of the problem and you find yourself never actually connecting with anyone.

Of course, it works the other way as well. This sort of self-doubt can lead to a deep need to seek approval and acceptance from others. You feel unlovable so you'll do anything to feel loved. This might mean being promiscuous and seeking acceptance in several partners, or letting a steady partner treat you badly because at least they are with you, giving you some sort of validation.

Many of us have a strong, confident friend who, in every other area of her life can confront anything, yet she puts up with atrocious behaviour from her partner because she's afraid of losing him or, worse, because she feels she doesn't deserve better. Again, such insecurities may stem from the core beliefs we developed growing up – beliefs we may not even be conscious of, like 'I'm not lovable,' or 'I need to look a certain way to feel good enough around others.' These core beliefs may even be lying dormant, and only triggered in early adulthood when we find ourselves in a relationship. It is often within relationships that our boundaries, values and self-esteem are exposed to us.

Should Seeing Be Believing?

So, the core beliefs we form early on in life play an important role in the way we choose to select and interpret what goes on later. We choose to focus on events that reflect the self-image we have constructed, and this can create a circularity of negative thinking. For example, if you've decided to wear a dress that accentuates your cleavage (which you are actually insecure about because it never achieved the mammoth proportions of your mother's and sister's) then you may interpret the laughter of teenagers on a bus as a direct result of the inadequacy of your cleavage instead of considering a number of more likely explanations. Your self-portrait as 'not well endowed' or 'not attractive enough' will be reinforced.

To complicate things further, these early negative core beliefs will be activated by information in the environment that has a link with them. If, for example, food was an emotive issue in your family, then mention of it in the context of anything related to the body will activate that negative core belief. Not surprisingly, when such core beliefs are activated, you are not immediately aware of your thoughts but rather of your feelings – which will be very highly charged.

At the core of our dissatisfaction with our bodies are all the shoulds and have-tos that we have been bombarded with while growing up. From fairytales to toilet-paper commercials, we are consistently told that beauty begets success and happiness. We are rarely faced with heroes, fictional or real, who aren't physically superior to the average person. From the weight we need to be, to the height we need to be, to how smooth our skin should look, there are value judgements placed on all aspects of our appearance that eventually come to serve as a wish list for our happiness. We develop an idea of what our ideal body should look like, and when we see the discrepancy between this ideal and our real body, we criticise ourselves, feel guilty and worthless. Since what society dictates and how others view us are important, we are often at our lowest in social situations. This is when we are likely to think negatively about our bodies and talk ourselves into despair. Before you know it the faulty patterns of reasoning kick in and you become one of the following:

- **Defensive: 'What do you mean you don't have my size? Are you saying I'm fat?'**

  This is problematic for several reasons. First, our reaction to an event, no matter how benign, will tend to be exaggerated and, in most cases, unnecessarily aggressive. This means that our interactions with others will become confusing and difficult. Second, a defensive stance means we often misinterpret the events around us. Third, people will eventually begin to avoid interacting with us for fear of accusations and reprisals when they do – in short, defensive people are hard work and not fun to be around.

- **Avoidant: 'I know I have free tickets to the première of the new Tom Cruise movie but I really do need to stay at home and bath my dog this evening.'**

This means distancing yourself from life and all it has to offer. Although avoidance seems like a solution to a problem, it can become a problem in and of itself, trapping us in our insecurities and feelings of inadequacy, and reinforcing the false belief that to avoid being hurt we should avoid things that can potentially make us happy.

- **Concealing: 'Hi, I need a new summer dress, where do you keep your tents these days?'**

In hiding behind clothes, or anything else for that matter, we are hiding aspects of ourselves that may be worth flaunting. We are also sending a message to ourselves that some parts of us aren't good enough to be displayed to other people, which may be damaging to our self-esteem and our body image.

- **Compulsive at correcting rituals: 'If I make sure my hair hangs over the sides of my face no one will notice my spots. I just have to remember to check every couple of minutes that it hasn't moved.'**

With this, our focus never leaves those aspects of our appearance that we don't like so our body language and our mannerisms are dictated by our appearance instead of just flowing naturally. It also most likely does the opposite of what we intend, which is to make whatever it is we are trying to hide more prominent to other people.

- **Reassurance-seeking: 'I look awful in this dress, don't I? My bum looks so big in it . . . Tell me the truth! You're embarrassed to be seen with me, aren't you? I'm a disgrace . . . go on, don't hold back, tell me what you think.'**

The problem with constantly seeking reassurance from others is twofold – first, we never learn to reassure ourselves, and thus learn an important lesson in maintaining a healthy body image; second, others rarely give us the type of reassurance we seek (not because they are being rude but because they can't read our minds), which means we are left feeling dissatisfied anyway.

Core beliefs result from a matrix of factors, including temperament, and dysfunctional interactions with parents, siblings and peers during early life. They tend to reflect ongoing, difficult experiences rather than singular events, and these experiences gradually accumulate to strengthen a given core belief. It's not so much that our past is inescapable, rather that most of us are never taught how to cope with putting it into perspective, so we carry negative comments, irrational beliefs and skewed world views with us until we finally discover that, no matter how accustomed we are to looking at the world in this way, it is just not working for us.

There are several reference points that most of us use when coming up with a mental model of our body image. It works something like this:

Reference points relating to things that we believe about ourselves (conscious or not)

These are made up of:

Ideals represented in the media, drawn from peers and family, i.e. manufactured pop star or model of the month.

Facts about our appearance, eye colour, height, etc.

Our 'internalised' ideal body, i.e. a compromise between the objective body and the ideal body that society says we should have.

Reference points relating to things that change daily

These are made up of:

Mood: *'Damn, I'm happy and I know I'm looking gooood'*, as opposed to *'What the hell did the stylist do to my hair! I look like Attila the Hun'*.

Social cues: *Someone compliments your choice of pashmina colour, as opposed to motions to you that you have spinach in your teeth.*

Negative thoughts: *'I really like the way these jeans make my legs look'*, as opposed to *'No one will ever want to propagate my genes because my bum is too big'*.

Interpretations and conclusions: *'They're staring at me because I look hot'*, as opposed to *'I'm so hot I'm sweating like a pig – I wonder if they can see the stains under my arms'*.

=

Our Body Image On Any Given Day

So that's how it works and you thought that mirrors were a simple matter of light bouncing off a shiny surface. The truth is what confronts you when you look in the mirror isn't just a reflection of the way you look but a reflection of your thoughts, emotions, fears and hopes – a reflection that will help you continue to build your portrait through your twenties and thirties right through to old age.

Twenty-thirty-somethings

The decades of your twenties and thirties have to be the most stressful in terms of having to accomplish, establish and define yourself. You need to work out what you're going to do as a career, where you're going to live and with whom, not to mention the fact that you'll probably have to make decisions about having kids and what your political views are. All in all, this is crunch time – adolescence was a dress rehearsal for figuring out that who you are, and learning that the way you see yourself can seriously affect how happy you are in life. Now comes the real stuff.

By this point you will have established a few core beliefs about yourself, based on your experiences while you were growing up. They may be lying dormant waiting to be activated by what happens to you as an adult. For example, if as a child and adolescent you were overweight and grew up with the core belief that people didn't like you because you were unattractive or unlovable then as an adult, even if you are now of normal weight, this core belief will still exist and may be activated by your experiences. For example, if you ask a guy to dance at a party and he says no, the core belief that you are unattractive and unlovable will be activated. You will bypass all other explanations for his refusal, such as he doesn't like dancing, has a girlfriend, is gay etc., etc. and focus only on your core negative belief. Core beliefs are so ingrained in us that they act as a map of our worldview; so any time something happens we can only explain it within the boundaries of this map.

Even though our core beliefs are formed, to a large extent, during our early development, we add to them later in life. Early in our twenties, a major part of our identity is bound up in what we are studying or work at. The more committed and happy we are with our view of ourselves within a particular career path, the happier we will be with our self-image. Consequently any negative thoughts that we hold about our body image will seem easier to deal with. You see, the sense of fulfilment and satisfaction we feel when we progress in our careers or social relationships may challenge unhelpful core beliefs we developed early on. Likewise, of course, the opposite also applies. If we are feeling unfulfilled it can serve to awaken dormant negative core beliefs we are unaware of or underscore others that we are conscious of.

Early adulthood is, of course, also the time when we become that little bit better at fooling around in the bedroom – much of the awkwardness of adolescent fumbling with bra straps and fluorescent condoms is overcome. By the time we've reached our late twenties, early thirties we are likely either to be in a serious relationship or trying to seek one out. The fact is that the happier we are (be it single or in a relationship), the happier we'll be with our bodies. But if we are single and dating, we are likely to be more socially and sexually critical of our bodies: our body awareness will be heightened so body image may once again creep up as a major concern.

Of course, for those in a relationship who decide to have a baby, well that's when the mother of all body-image concerns pops up. Your body is literally out of your control, changing and growing daily, your girth (a word that you never thought you'd use) will have expanded to unimaginable proportions. Your breasts are enormous but not in a glamorous, page 3 sort of way, more like a 'middle-aged matron of a girls' school' sort of way. And for those who think that once the baby is born you can revert to normal, ha! There's a joke! Stretch marks, pigmentation stains and a flabby belly will be there to remind you that your body just ain't what it used to be. Interestingly, women who were thin before they became pregnant report feeling more dissatisfied with their bodies than larger women who feel more positive during pregnancy and afterwards. This relates not just to the changes in our bodies, but also to what being a parent means to us. As we have seen so far, our self-image is bound up in the beliefs we hold about particular roles or types of people. So, if to you being a parent means becoming more adult, less fun and maybe even less sexually attractive, this will affect the way you see yourself, and how you react to your partner and those around you. As with any life transition, you need to separate society's *have-tos* with what feels comfortable and right for you.

By the time you've battled with the pimply demons of adolescence and tried to navigate your way through the social minefield that is early adulthood and parenthood, you might think you've earned a well-deserved rest. Alas! you have middle age, the menopause and mid-life crises to look forward to . . .

Growing Old Gracefully

*A*fter spending most of the weekend ignoring my sister's phone messages – 'Just calling to see what happened at the dating agency. Amelia said she was worried that your video message was slightly inaccurate' – I decided I needed some fresh air and went for a walk up to the high street. I popped into Boots for some eye-makeup remover when I was accosted by a woman dressed in a fake white doctor's coat brandishing a pink tube. 'This, my dear,' she said, 'will wipe away those crow's feet, frown lines and laughter wrinkles like nobody's business.' My initial reaction wasn't one of elation at the miracle her pink tube promised since I had never actually realised that emotions and birdlife had caused so much damage to my face. However, I continued to listen as she explained that, while it might have been OK to walk around with days' old mascara on my face in my twenties and thirties, now I was nearing my forties—

'I'm thirty-two!' I said, glaring at her.

'Yes, of course you are, dear,' she continued, 'my point is that you need to take care of your skin if you want to look young.'

'Why would I want to look young?' I asked, more out of boredom than anything else.

'Well, dear, a woman needs to look young and beautiful if she's going to feel good about herself and confident – and, I might add, to keep her man happy. Take me, for instance. I'm fifty-seven, but most people say I don't look a day over thirty-five, because I put in the hard work and effort.' As I listened to 'Cilla', the fifty-seven-year-old thirty-five-year-old *look-alike in the fake doctor's coat, go on about her philosophy of life and perverted feminist ideals, it struck me that I was surrounded by bottles, tubes and jars filled with the insecurities that Cilla and the rest of us carry around. Growing old was scary – maybe even scarier than the fat on my belly or the cellulite on my thighs. It wasn't just that wrinkles told of the fact that you'd been around for a while, it was more that there seemed nowhere else to go from there. Being old means, 'You've had your turn, now move over and let someone else have a go.' It means, 'You're not easy on the eye any more so you'd better have something really interesting to say if you're going to hold my attention.' It means you don't matter as much as you used to because you are no longer in the correct age bracket. And, worst of all, growing old is inevitable, so once you've reached Cilla's age you'd better either look younger or go into hibernation because your value will have plummeted by then. I continued to listen to Cilla sing the praises of her pearly pink tube. By the time I left the shop I had purchased enough cosmetics to ensure that my face and body would be plastered for months, not just because Cilla had put the fear of god into me but because I wanted to let her know that she was good at something else, other than looking thirty-five years old.*

Although men and women experience many similar body changes during the ageing process – wrinkled skin, thinning hair, loss of energy – the way they deal with them is what sets them apart. From childhood, women are brought up to care about their appearance and accept that we will be valued in terms of our ability to look youthful and attractive. We are handed 'perfect' dolls and story-book princesses, and begin to assume that they are the 'typical' ideal. For hundreds of years women have been taught that their most important contribution to others is to look good. With the advent of equal rights, women may have been allowed into the voting booths and boardrooms, but most, if they're honest, are still tempted when a sales assistant thrusts the newest time-defying moisturising cream in their faces, if they feel it will help them hold on to their youth and looks. We need to feel like we're keeping up. Think about it. If we see a swanky older man swaggering down the street with a girl who you would probably assume was his daughter, or even granddaughter if it wasn't for the handholding, most of us don't bat an eyelid. We can see why he would be attracted to her. Equally, because men are valued differently from women, we assume that the young woman is attracted to him because of his accomplishments, predictably financial, or his wisdom, despite his lack of obvious physical allure. These qualities don't age, or vanish with time. Male film stars are still seen as sex symbols well into middle age – Harrison Ford and Sean Connery are still viewed as some of the sexiest men on the planet, despite having been around for over half a century. Yet most of Hollywood's top female earners are in their twenties, possibly thirties. It seems that the movie industry won't accept that although a woman may lose her youthful looks, she can still be a talented performer. So, for a woman who has been valued throughout life in terms of her youth and beauty, the facts of the ageing process can be extremely distressing.

We all know a forty-year-old woman who still dresses like a teenager. She hangs out in nightclubs and bars, with over-bleached hair, thick black eyeliner and shimmery frosted-pink lip-gloss. She still dances around her handbag because that's what she did when she was young. This is the female mid-life crisis. Because women are taught that their power, their contribution, is in their sex appeal and youth, some cling desperately to their younger days, rather than conforming to the cliché of 'growing old gracefully'. This type of woman's core belief was then most likely reinforced by the fact that as she invested in her looks, paying extra attention to hair, makeup and clothes, men responded to this investment. However, because the core belief that her value lay only in her youth and beauty was never challenged she now, many years later, sees no other qualities within herself worth valuing or using to interact with others. Her portrait, as she sees it, was at its best when she was seventeen, so that's who she will be from now on. She falls back on tried and tested measures to make people like her and to like herself.

Research has shown that most women are aware of the mutton-dressed-as-lamb syndrome, and want to achieve a balance between that and giving in to their age or settling for 'dowdiness'. They also acknowledge that there is a thin line between each category. But it is hard to accept that youthful beauty is a fleeting gift. It's great while it lasts – it can command attention and boost our self-esteem – but ultimately it fades, and the most successful older women are those who are aware that they have a million other qualities and contributions to offer. They have learnt to relate to men on a level that is far removed from a lustful leer or an appreciative comment in a nightclub. True acceptance of the ageing process involves interacting with men as equals.

Pause for Thought

Often, decline in the health of our body image is strongly linked to a physiological change in our body. As well as wrinkles, loss of strength and beauty, women also have to go through the menopause. It is hardly surprising that women have such a tough time coming to terms with this change, when you consider that the Victorian gynaecologist Tilt described it as a disease, calling it the 'dodging time'. It has also been called the 'deficiency disease', due to the low levels of oestrogen during and after it.

In recent years, society has come to accept the menopause as just another change in life, like adolescence, but many women still feel anxious about it. As in adolescence, their bodies may be out of their control. Hair may sprout in places where it wasn't expected, there are hot flushes and muscles soften. For many women, nothing feels 'right'.

Also, it has greater implications. A woman may not have planned to have another child, but it can be a shock to realise that she no longer has the choice, which may have an impact on her sexuality: she may see her body as 'useless', and even 'undesirable'. Studies have shown that there is no physiological reason why a woman should stop enjoying sex after the menopause, but if negative self-image core beliefs have been formed as a result of the body changes, it is unlikely that she will feel sexy.

However, men do not sail through the ageing process, handling every change calmly and rationally. Oh, no! The male mid-life crisis is often talked about and, just as often, laughed about. Admittedly, over the last twenty years, it has been taken more seriously, and rightly so. Middle age brings to men a new vulnerability. It relates to a sense of missed opportunities or failed ambitions. Just as women are valued for their looks, men are valued for their achievements. For a man, middle age might bring regret that he never had his dream career, or earned enough to buy a yacht; he never had the chance to be the most popular or the best-looking. So like the frosted-pink lip-gloss his purchase of a shiny new sports car may be his attempt to cling to youth, and assert a certain power.

In terms of physical changes, research shows that men are less worried about weight gain than women, they're happy to grow a beer belly, or develop a few 'laughter lines'. They seem less concerned about wrinkles too. But there is one thing that upsets them: hair loss. Subconsciously, men feel it represents loss of power and virility. As a menopausal woman is no longer able to produce children, the menopausal man may feel he can no longer produce at work, and in his sexual and social relationships.

To some extent, therefore, the male menopause is essentially a sexual problem, which has been bolstered by the possibility of hormone replacement. This reinforces the idea that menopausal males are only anxious about their libido when in fact they may question their role and desirability too. Men can also grow to hate their bodies as they lose control of the way they look, and become aware that no matter how many times people say grey hair is 'distinguished', they simply cannot command the same attention from the opposite sex. However, they are likely to have reached an age where they are financially secure, which explains the acquisition of objects such as the brand-new car and the brand-new girlfriend.

Breaking Up and Growing Apart

I remember when my aunt Cecilia got divorced. She and Uncle Fred had been married for ever and they seemed happy when I saw them at family gatherings, and then one day they just got divorced. Apparently Uncle Fred had started an affair with what my mother called a floozy from London, whom he decided to leave my aunt for. For a while none of us knew what to do. Aunt Cecilia was devastated. She criticised the floozy for hours on end on the phone with my mother – apparently her skirts were way too short, her hair much too long and blonde, and her breasts, well, my mum just said they were a very rude size.

Then one day, a couple of months after Uncle Fred moved out, we went to visit my aunt. When she opened the door we all stood there stunned – except for my dad, who looked particularly pleased to see her and rushed over to give her an inappropriately long hug. She had clearly lost a lot of weight and was wearing a short red mini-skirt, tight black blouse and far too much makeup. Her previously comfy Clarks sandals had been replaced with spiked heels, and she either had on a wig or some really bad blonde extensions. We all shuffled into her kitchen where she offered us tea and home-made scones in the same nice, warm way she always had. My mother, who was clearly unable to contain her horror any longer, asked why she was dressed like that. 'Like what?' snapped Aunt Cecilia.

'You know, like that!' said my mother, gesticulating to her skirt and scrunching up her nose.

Aunt Cecilia put down the yellow tea-cosy and turned on her spiked heel. 'Fred left me,' she said, 'he left because I wasn't as sexy or as pretty or as skinny as the floozy from London. If I'm going to stand a chance of getting him back I need to become attractive to him again.'

I'll never forget how sorry I felt for her but also how guilty because I kept thinking she was probably right – if she'd taken as much time over her appearance as she had over her scones then everything would have been fine. As my mother tried to reassure her that he'd left because of his own issues and my father, unhelpfully, kept pointing out how great she looked in a low-cut top and that many men would

find her attractive, my sister and I snuck out of the kitchen and into
the garden where we vowed to stay as pretty as possible for as long
as possible . . .

Just as physiological changes such as the menopause – male or female – can affect the way we feel about our bodies, emotional turmoil also plays a major part. Successful, healthy relationships can improve our body image, helping us to feel comfortable with our reflection and to accept that although we may not conform to society's ideal this doesn't render us unlovable. A divorce, separation or break-up can destroy this confidence. Alternatively, when we leave an unhealthy relationship, our self-esteem can be in tatters. Or we feel that we need the security of that relationship: no one else will want us because we are unattractive.

When someone walks out on us, we start to question why. And, aside from aspects of our personality, we immediately wonder if they left because 'I'm too fat' or 'I look too old.' This could be especially common in someone who has already developed negative core beliefs about their appearance. Those old 'fat girl' or 'pizza-face' taunts may come flooding right back into the picture. This is especially common when a partner has left for a younger, more attractive model. When a husband speeds out of the drive in his new sports car, with his new ear stud and twenty-year-old girlfriend, often the wife left behind will not see the possibility of his mid-life crisis, just the message: 'I wasn't beautiful enough.' People leave relationships for a variety of reasons, but when we are at our lowest, often we can only see one.

This presents us with a number of challenges in establishing a new relationship. If we change ourselves, because we feel we were left because we weren't desirable enough, we may try to mask ourselves with makeup, hair dye and a Wonderbra. It's rather like applying a plaster to a wound: if you look underneath, the injury is still there. However, if you can see your value as an individual, even though your ex-partner cannot, it will lead you to a new and healthy relationship, perhaps with someone else but almost certainly with yourself.

At certain times in life, our body seems to be working against us. In fact, during adolescence we may feel as if our body has declared war on us – setting traps and playing tricks. Alongside this there is the trauma of first dates and, inevitably, rejections. It is easy to blame our body. 'If I had bigger breasts, he'd say yes.' We may begin to hate our face, we become sure that if it wasn't for the acne we'd have more friends.

Even as we grow older and wiser, these negative core beliefs are still lurking. When we go through another self-esteem-damaging life experience – for example, a relation-ship break-up – they leap to the forefront of our minds. 'It's because you're ugly!' they scream. 'He wouldn't have left you if you didn't look so old.' We need to take apart these core beliefs and see them for what they are, usually complete rubbish.

How can we edit our self-portrait so that we learn to love the person who stares back at us from the mirror? Well, it's all about becoming aware of our core beliefs and how they affect our perception of ourselves and our lives. It's about putting thoughts and feelings into perspective to highlight how irrational they are. Instead of gazing in despair at your love handles or cellulite try asking your-self, 'Are my love handles *really* the only thing stopping me finding my dream mate?' or 'How important is the cellulite on my thighs *really*?' Where did the belief that cellulite will doom you to a life of unhappiness come from? If we don't become aware of the thoughts and beliefs that are negatively affecting our lives, we will no doubt grow to feel worse about ourselves as our negativity becomes further and further established.

Like it or not, your body will change, and it won't send you a polite letter requesting permission. Before you know it, you'll have breasts, pubic hair, hips and puppy fat – or wrinkles, flabby arms and grey hair. The advertising industry might promise it can slow ageing or save the world but, really, there's very little anyone can do to stop or even control these changes. So we might as well work with our body, because it sure as hell isn't going to do as we say. We need to acknowledge the changes. It's too easy to blame your body for everything and let yourself off the hook, when the only way to feel good about yourself is to hold to account the *real* you – inside.

TAKE AWAYS

By now you should be able to identify your negative thoughts and be trying to challenge them. This chapter has examined how our perception of ourselves develops. From the first messages we get from our parents about being 'good' or 'bad' to our nickname in college, we explored the building blocks that form our body image and self-esteem, and how they affect the self-portrait we construct. For you to challenge effectively the negative beliefs you hold about yourself and the world, you need to know where they came from. These exercises involve understanding why you see yourself as you do. Here you will explore where your core beliefs about yourself, good and bad, originated, then decide whether or not you want to keep them.

TASK 1

Now, let's see how you draw your portrait and how the people and circumstances in your life have affected it.

Task 2.1 is divided into two sections. In the Real Me section write the qualities that best describe how you see yourself today. Be as objective as possible. Focus on your body and your personality. In the 'Ideal Me' section focus on what you want to be rather than what you are, physically and psychologically. The lists can be as long or as short as you like, as long as they are honest.

TASK 2.1

REAL ME   IDEAL ME

_____   _____

_____   _____

_____   _____

_____   _____

_____   _____

_____   _____

_____   _____

_____   _____

_____   _____

_____   _____

_____   _____

Now consider the differences between the two sections. Ask yourself where the words in the Ideal Me column came from. Think about what experiences have led you to believe that these qualities are desirable. Also ask yourself if they are realistic for you.

_____

_____

If yes, why do you think they would make you a better or more complete person? If no, why are they on the list?

_____

_____

Over the next week spend some time every morning focusing on the things you love about yourself (you may want to dig out the list from chapter 1's exercise). Make a point of doing this every morning, and perhaps try using clothes to accentuate your favourite physical features. At the end of the week complete Table 2.1 again. Is it different this time?

_____

Why – or why not? (What you're doing is challenging the way you draw your portrait by starting to work on those negative thoughts and core beliefs that have dictated how you've seen yourself for so long.)

_____

_____

TASK 2

1. Find your favourite and least favourite childhood photos and describe them below.

_____

_____

_____

_____

2. Make a list of reasons why these are your favourite and least favourite pictures.

_____

_____

_____

_____

_____

3. Now do the same with your favourite and least favourite photos as an adult.

4. Compare the language that you used between the four. Did you find that you were more critical of the adult you? Was there more emphasis on weight in your judgements of the adult photos? Did remarks that others have made (you may want to refer to the list from chapter 1) crop up in your description of yourself?

5. Take the list and (no matter how silly you feel) talk to the child you in the photo, using the negative language you chose as an adult to describe her/him.

6. How does it feel? Probably not very nice, because no child should be spoken to like that. But, if so, why do you think it's acceptable to talk about the adult you in that way?

7. Put the pictures away for a few days. Then return to them and describe what you see again, bearing in mind how you felt when you did it the first time. As you assimilate different views of yourself, you will begin to integrate them into your body image.

Chapter Three
FOOD, GLORIOUS FOOD

G ot home with six Tesco bags in one hand and a half-eaten Snickers bar in the other. I plonked down, hyperventilating, on the sofa, after climbing the three flights of stairs up to my flat. As I watched the fish fingers and Pot Noodles tumble out of the bags, I felt a sense of gratitude to all those wonderful imaginary friends, relatives and seamen who cook for me – Uncle Ben, Sara Lee, Mr Kipling and, of course, good old Captain Birdseye. If it wasn't for them I'd be eating toast for dinner every night.

The phone rang and I tried to move it telepathically from across the room before giving up and lunging for it. It was Amy, a Californian girl Trudy had met on her course and introduced me to. She was having a dinner party and was calling to invite me. She asked me if I was vegetarian – no; vegan – no; lactose intolerant – no; had any gastrointestinal sensitivities to wheat – uh . . . no. Did I eat carbs? Yes. Refined flour? Yes. Refined sugar? Yum. Apart from the Spanish-inquisition style interrogation into my dietary needs she seemed really nice and I told her I looked forward to seeing her at her dinner party at the weekend. I put the phone down and went into the kitchen to unpack my groceries.

I opened the fridge and pushed the Weight Watchers meals aside to make room for my new 'Be Good to Yourself' shepherd's pie, the fresh pasta and the 'light Greek-style' yoghurts. In the cupboard I piled the Pot Noodles on top of my Slimfast shakes. As I reached *into the back of the cupboard, dozens of tomato-soup sachets tumbled out, bringing back memories of the ridiculous tomato diet I tried before I applied for my current job. I remember wanting to lose twenty pounds before the interview and going on a tomato binge for two weeks. By the end of it I smelt like ketchup and my skin had turned a pale green shade. To this day I can't get with ten feet of tomato purée without gagging. But I managed to lose enough weight to clinch the interview at the marketing firm – lucky, really, because I piled it back on a couple of weeks later. Beside the soup sachets and behind the family-sized Quality Street box, I found three diet books I had stashed away – one singing the praises of cabbages, another of proteins and the other of basically not eating anything after 3.00 p.m.*

As I looked around at the contents of my cupboards I realised I could track my life based on (a) whether or not I was dieting, and (b) which diet I had been on. There was the meat-eating diet during that rough patch with ex-boyfriend Josh, the three glasses of water before every meal diet before the scuba-diving holiday in Mexico, and the David Blaine diet, which entailed, well, basically starving myself for as long as possible, minus the Perspex box.

It occurred to me that each time I had gone on a diet the intention had been either to prepare for or cope with something. It was as if the diets were going to deliver a new shiny me that would make easier whatever I was preparing for. One by one, though, they each made me feel more of a failure and eventually I just gave up on them.

I put a pork pie on a plate and sat at the kitchen table. This time, I thought to myself, I would get it right; I would stick to the diet and make James notice me. As soon as I'd finished my pork pie, I would begin.

Our relationship with food has to be one of the most emotionally charged, satisfying yet guilt-ridden relationships we have in our lives. From the time our mother rewards us with a biscuit for being a good girl to the first time you invite a man up for that proverbial 'cup of coffee', food really is a metaphor for all that we feel and many times all that we can't quite say. No surprise, therefore, that most of us stress about it so much.

In the last two decades the diet industry has become so powerful that up to 70 per cent of women report being on a diet at any given time. So, does this mean we all have an eating disorder?

Most women don't suffer with eating disorders, just an unhealthy preoccupation with food, regardless of their weight. Unfortunately, though, the language used by many in the health and diet industries has served to make us feel sick or abnormal about the way we eat. We are made to feel weak about being tempted by things called Death by Chocolate, and self-denial, in the hardcore Catholic sense, is viewed as healthy. We feel we have to justify every mouthful we take by running off a history of what we've eaten in the last three days, and why? All because we are aspiring to a body or, more to the point, a body image that, in reality, only a minuscule proportion of the female population will ever conform to.

Food is such an emotive subject precisely because of its relationship to our body image. From the moment we make the connection that what we eat affects how we look, food is no longer a source of energy to keep us alive: it becomes our ally and our enemy, our comfort and our downfall all rolled into one. The relationship we have with food provides insights into our core beliefs about body image and in most cases the healthier the latter, the healthier the former.

A Healthy Diet?

You can't talk about food without talking about diets – the bane of many a woman's existence. The problem with diets, other than the fact that we have to deny ourselves the joy of chocolate cake and fry-ups, is that we don't look at them for what they are: we build them into life-changing miracles. And when eating only protein for a month doesn't bring us the supermodel husband, the two-seater sports car and the three-fold pay rise, frankly, we feel let down. That's if we even get to the stage where we begin to lose weight. Most of us give up long before that. We stumble at the first hurdle, whether that be a dinner date, a Sunday roast or a bar of chocolate in the newsagent's. Even when we fall off the dieting merry-go-round, no matter how disappointed we feel, no matter how grazed our knees and our self-esteem, most of us hop straight back on again, ready for the next ride.

It's sad but true that on-off dieting lessens our self-esteem and makes us feel worse about our weight. In fact, dieting makes us 'feel fat'. Why do we keep trying? Some psychologists say it is because of how the 'right body' is rewarded. We keep trying because we want the feelings of power, self-confidence and even femininity that weight loss often brings. We feel rewarded when we receive opposite-sex attention, or are viewed more positively in social situations. We long for these things, we love them when we have them, so we keep trying to attain them. Funnily enough, we aren't very good at knowing what weight we are. A survey of college students found that the vast majority of women overestimated their weight. It also found that most women wanted to lose weight, over three-quarters had dieted before and nearly half said that they dieted most of the time. College, and our late teens, is a particularly tough time when it comes to feeling judged by society, fitting in, and establishing relationships. Ironically, we often assume the best way to smooth this process is to lose weight. And this thought pattern sticks with us through life. Everybody wants the 'right body'.

We live in a culture obsessed with being slim, and therefore obsessed with dieting.

It's estimated that at least 95 per cent of women diet at some point in their lives, even though reams of research has shown that dieting only works for around 5 per cent of non-obese slimmers.

So why can't we make it work? How can all those reformed overweight people in the adverts stand there with the vast 'jeans I used to wear' smugly swamping them, when it seems impossible for the rest of us to muster the willpower to refuse a biscuit? What is the key to winning the diet battle?

Step One: ask yourself why you are doing it

The truth is that, like most things to do with our body image, a lot of us see weight loss as a means of getting other things we want in life, a relationship, a better job or even more self-confidence. Ask yourself if losing weight *will* bring you these things or if there are other ways to obtain them. This is important, because if you pin your aspirations on a certain weight or dress size, and you fail to reach it you will feel that it's impossible to achieve your aspirations. If you see losing weight for what it is – losing weight – then any failure to achieve it will not be tied into your self-identity as strongly, allowing you to feel OK about yourself and eventually to try again. Also, you may not be trying to lose weight for yourself but for someone else. This is a definite no-no: you want to feel better about yourself and if that 'better you' is defined by anyone other than 'you', you'll resent the diet and ultimately the person whose idea it was.

Step Two: begin the diet without setting yourself up to fail

Starting the newest diet and failing to keep it up can be just as damaging to the way we feel about our bodies as a flabby tummy. And most of the time diets do fail, for two main reasons. First, we're not realistic enough: we decide, *That's it, we're dieting!* But we fail to look at the factors that might get in the way of this. A five-foot-eleven, large-framed woman will never look like Kylie Minogue. A four-foot small-framed guy will never look like Arnold Schwarzenegger. There is no harm in having aspirations, but when they apply less to who we are and more to what celeb is currently in vogue, we set ourselves up for disappointment. We can slim down, we can tone up, but we can't transform years of genetic history that have determined our height and build.

When we embark on a new diet, we need to take into account all the factors that will affect our weight loss and stand in the way of that 'Perfect Size Ten' dream. Our build, height, metabolism and lifestyle all play a part, and we need to remember the impact they will have on our expectations of our diet. Often when we give up we see diets as a waste of time because, realistically, they can't give us the body we want. At best, they can help us become a healthier version of ourselves but they will never turn us into Naomi Campbell's twin sister.

The second reason diets fail is because we go for the quick fix. We want to lose a lot of weight *now* and keep it off *for ever* with as *little* effort as possible. The truth is that quick-fix diets rarely work, and when they do, they're so drastic that it's hard to adhere to them for an extended period. What really works is healthier eating and exercising throughout your life, not for six or eight weeks or whatever the newest diets promise. That way you look healthier and feel healthier for a long, long time.

Step Three: have realistic expectations of the diet

As I mentioned earlier, the belief of many dieters is that if they have the 'right body' they'll get the right life. The reality is that the two don't go hand in hand, and if, as the pounds slip off, the life accomplishments don't keep up, then feelings of failure will set in and eventually being on that diet will seem harder than ever, and giving up will seem like a relief. Our expectations of diets can be so far-fetched that many of us use them as a form of time travel. As soon as we start one we begin to buy clothes in a smaller size or make travel and social plans to fit our new future with our new svelte body. We do this because we just can't wait to see the person the diet will allow us to become. But the fact is that by projecting ourselves into the future we

(a) are not allowing ourselves to focus on the present, thus giving the diet the best chance to work; and

(b) are setting up expectations that may be so far in the future we will be oblivious to the small gains we make in the short term and therefore unable to feel good about ourselves because of them.

The only way to approach a diet is to see it for what it is – a healthy lifestyle change not a seminal life-changing moment that will transform every aspect of our existence. So, live in the here and now, buy new clothes when you need them, make plans that you'll enjoy at any size, validate yourself for the person you are today, not for the person that you hope to be in six weeks' time. That way pride is gained by sticking to your goals – your realistic, measurable goals – and not in some MTV-style fantasy where you and your body ride off into the sunset with the man, the money and the success.

Step Four: make peace with food

After we've heard about a new diet on television, bought the book and the food, pinned up the wall-chart in the kitchen, we've walked into a lose-lose situation. If we don't lose weight, it's all been a waste of time and money. And if we do lose weight, the next challenge is keeping it off, and most people don't. Once we start seeing results, it's easy to become a little slack. Eventually the wall-chart comes down, and the chocolate reappears. Or if the rate at which we are slimming slows, as it tends to, we feel as if we are failing and give up anyway. So, if we don't lose weight, we fail. If we do lose weight, we're bound to put it back on, so we fail.

The only way to combat this is to make peace with food: don't see it as the enemy, but likewise don't see it as some near-orgasmic divine experience. The fact is that we are all taught that food has an emotional value: we are *good* when we stick to diets and we are *naughty* when we slip up. Whether we have a weight problem or not, many of us see food as a form of comfort or reward. The only way to get round this is for us to strike a balance with regard to how we eat and think about food. If you do 'slip up' with a bar of chocolate, don't beat yourself up about it: it isn't the end of the world and, most likely, has not done irreparable damage to your diet. Just tell yourself that now you've enjoyed it, you will try to focus on your diet goal again and do your best to stick to it. On a mental level, don't make chocolate an object of either dread or desire. It's a yummy snack, that's all. If you're convinced, once in a while, that your tastebuds need a yummy snack, go for it. Just don't turn it into some huge reward or guilt trip. The more you are able to separate food from emotion, the more successful you will be with your dieting.

The Guilt and Language of Dieting

*M*onday morning: at work surfing the Net. Too stressed to do any work – trying to figure out how I'm going to get James to notice me. Discover site called Fab Fashion and order three new tops, two skirts and a dress in size twelve. (Even though am still nowhere near a size twelve, am convinced I will be very soon. Have started new diet that both the cast of Friends and the cast of Will and Grace swear by so it's bound to work.) Just as I'm about to look up Jennifer Aniston's style tips on Google I notice Mark (not-so-cute guy who works with James) hanging around my desk. He always seems to sneak up on me asking weird questions about stationery. I can feel him peering over my shoulder and before I can switch the screen off I hear him say, 'Oh, that's a nice dress.'

'It's research for a new campaign.'

'Oh . . . Well, you'd look really nice in it anyway . . . Um, do you need any fluorescent Post-its? They just put some green and pink ones in the stationery cupboard.'

'No thanks, I'm fine.'

He smiles, winks twice (I think he has a nervous twitch) and walks away.

I feel my stomach grumbling, look at my watch and calculate that I have three hours and fifteen minutes until my lunch break. Try and psych myself up by chanting 'You're doing this for James – to lose fat and be beautiful are your aims!' But somehow it isn't helping – I can feel my stomach crying out for food. I reach into my drawer where I keep my stash of junk food and start sniffing a packet of cheese puffs. They smell delicious – as long as I don't eat them I can enjoy the smell of their orange, cheesy yumminess – I duck underneath my desk so that I can get a really good whiff and I'm interrupted by a man's voice above me. 'Um, Sarah?'

'No fluorescent Post-its! Thank you!' I snap – and lift my head to see James standing over me. 'Uh, sorry . . . What do you want?'

'I just need you to approve these . . . uhm, you have something orange in your nose.'

I'm mortified as I ease the cheese snack out of my left nostril, all I want to do is crawl back under my desk and disappear – am certain James thinks I'm a moron and that no amount of dieting can rectify the vision he has just been confronted with. As a means of ending the indignity of it all, I grab the papers from his hand and tell him angrily that he can go now. He leaves with that same confused look on his face that he so often has when we speak and I sink into my chair cursing the maize snack industry.

A big problem with dieting is the language we use when we're wrapped up in it. Words concerned with loss, denial and deprivation become the pillars of our vocabulary. No wonder we feel negative about it.

For many of us, our relationship with food was formed long before we were even aware of what 'diet' meant. From childhood we teach ourselves, and are taught by others, to bargain with food. Mothers tell their children, 'As you've been so good today, you can have an ice-cream.' So, food is tied in with our behaviour and emotions. When we are younger we associate being good with being given food. That's where those core beliefs derive from. Getting ice-cream as a reward places a value on it much higher than that of frozen milk. It becomes a decadence that we should only allow ourselves on rare occasions when we are being very, very good. This core belief stays with us, and as we get older we use food to comfort ourselves when we are down.

Paradoxically, as we get older we begin to associate being good with denying ourselves food. Our core belief is adapted so that we think we're being good when we starve ourselves, and to reward ourselves we eat. This schizophrenic relationship with food means that we never see food for the simple thing it is – and until we do we won't be able either to enjoy or have a healthy relationship with it.

So, how do we separate a ham and cheese toastie from emotion? Well, one of the most important steps is to take away the guilt and power from food. Eating the recommended daily allowance of fruit and vegetables does not make you a good person. Stuffing your face with chocolate cake doesn't make you a bad one. Rather than thinking you are headed for a torture of fat-free lunches and low-calorie dinners, concentrate on what you are achieving for yourself. Don't think, It's so unfair that I can't have a massive fry-up. Instead think, I am worth more than a big pile of grease on a plate. My body deserves better, I deserve better. Don't diet to become a different 'you': eat healthily to become a healthier 'you'. That way, you can see food positively, as gaining something, rather than as a constant routine of denial.

Snatching the power away from food is easier said than done. The key is to break the link it has with your emotions. Don't depend on food, don't reinforce core beliefs that say, 'Food is something decadent to reward myself with'. Don't allow it to boost or ruin your mood. Stop yourself when you find yourself muttering, 'I could really do with a Chinese takeaway to cheer me up.' If you want the takeaway, have it, but challenge the belief that you need it as an emotional pick-me-up. A spring roll doesn't have the capacity to solve your problems. The only reason you feel better after you've eaten it is because you've given yourself a treat – you have valued yourself. Of course, half an hour later you're hungry again *and* the reason you were down has probably resurfaced. Now, if you could value yourself in more positive ways, such as meeting friends to talk about what's worrying you, making some time to do things that you love to do as opposed to things you have to do, even watching your favourite TV programme, then not only will you feel better but this feeling will be sustained. You see, it's important to break the lifelong habit of using food to reward or punish yourself, because, again, it links your thoughts and feelings with food.

Death by Chocolate

For many dieters, especially women, one food is a constant stumbling block. No matter how many packets of crisps, burgers or pies they manage to avoid and deny themselves, there's one thing that is guaranteed to bring them to their knees. Maybe all it takes is an advert with a beautiful girl bathing in the stuff to make us run down to the shops. Or just the smell of it on a colleague's breath that has us sprinting to the vending machine. No, we're not talking about baked beans here. Chocolate is every dieter's nightmare. To an extent all food is linked not only with an essential need to fuel the body, but with deep cultural roots and chocolate is a great example of this.

Since its discovery in 1492, chocolate has enjoyed a special place in our cultural values that no other food can come close to. It is tied so closely to our emotions that it appears at almost every cornerstone of life. When we want to say thank you, we do it with chocolate. When we're picked up for a first date, we're given chocolate. If our date wants to cover our body in something delicious, they use chocolate (OK, Nutella, but it's still chocolaty). When we've been dumped, our best friend consoles us with chocolate. It's seen as one of woman's greatest pleasures yet also as one of her biggest sins.

Some people have suggested that we have this strange relationship with chocolate because of these cultural ties and the fact that its ingredients affect levels of the body's mood-affecting chemicals. One of these chemicals is phenylethylamine, which the body releases in response to romance, so next time you hear somebody exclaim that they 'love' chocolate, perhaps there is more to it. Chocolate is a good example of our complex relationship with food because it is something that we feel we deserve, but feel guilty about eating. Again, the problem here is that we allow the food to have too much power. We justify our need for chocolate because we feel depressed, or lovesick etc., etc. We establish a link between what we jam into our mouths and how we feel on the inside. See it for what it is – a pleasure we don't need but enjoy. And don't attach such guilt to it: we know that, in a sensible diet, there's no such thing as a 'bad' food, so if you want some chocolate then go for it.

Taking away the power from food sounds like a good principle, but how do you live by it? Here are some tips:

1. **Eat what you want.** Really, eat what you want. There's no reason why you shouldn't eat something *as long as you are aware of why you want it so much.* So if you come home from work and you feel like attaching your mouth to the fridge and guzzling for five hours, just stop for a minute and ask yourself why. Perhaps you've had an awful day at work. Well, that's fine, everyone has bad days. But then think about how the problem and your solution actually fit together. Is eating the contents of the top two shelves of your refrigerator really going to sort out your problems at work? If so (and I can't imagine why it would), go for it. If not, think of what *will* help. Looking at the problem in this way often helps us to think about whether we are eating because we want to eat or because something else is wrong.

2. **Don't make food your only source of comfort.** Food is often our first source of comfort when we're feeling down. We crave comfort food for physiological reasons, such as a low blood–sugar level. Certain foods increase serotonin, the chemical substance in our brains that allows us to feel happy. But often the reasons are psychological, and it really helps to distance yourself for a minute

and think about why you actually want the food. It may be that you want to avoid a particular issue, or that your only coping strategy for dealing with a difficult issue is eating. But using food as comfort minimises other, possibly more effective and helpful, ways to cope with problems and creates an unhealthy belief in your mind that food is your only source of comfort.

3. **Deprivation doesn't work.** If the one thing you have forbidden yourself is cream cake, then guess what you are going to long for, more than anything else in the world? Cream cake. By blacklisting certain foods, you're putting far too much pressure on yourself and, ultimately, setting yourself up for failure. Don't make foods good or bad: accept that everything is OK in moderation. Bear in mind exactly what you want to achieve with your diet. Do you really want to learn how to banish certain foods from your life for ever? Probably not, so don't waste time turning food into the enemy or, conversely, a trophy. Your diet needs to be a lifestyle change. It's not good enough to change the food you eat: you need to change the way you think. Accept that a piece of chocolate cake isn't going to kill you, but it might be an idea to halve it and throw the rest away. Look at the power of food realistically.

4. **Stick to your guns.** Now, there is a difference between starving yourself and adopting a healthier way of eating. So if you do decide that it's time for a change in the way you eat, be strong about it. Be confident about your decision, because if you're not, you are likely to give up and you will end up feeling worse about the situation. We've all been there. We decide that this diet is the one. This will be the one to succeed where so many before have failed. We approach the new regime with gusto and enthusiasm. Until that first lunch date with the girls. Where we try to order soup, or a dressing-free salad, but then somebody pipes up, 'Oh come on, what difference will one steak make?!' That's it. Game, set, match

to the Steak Diane. If you feel that your diet will make you healthier and happier, then lead your normal life but be clear about your convictions. Many of the most effective diets will allow you a day or two off anyway. Use those days to meet friends who might try to persuade you out of it. Just remind them that if this really is something you need to do, you would appreciate their support. And if you slip up, then don't let that make you feel that the whole thing is pointless. Don't give up because of one little chocolate bar. Or bag of crisps. Or pork pie. Etc., etc.

Just as it is important to break the link between our emotions and food, we also need to break the link between our successes and failures in life and the things we shove into our mouths. The car we drive, the job we do and the success of our relationship aren't linked to our diet. When we decide to diet, we should understand that these things probably won't change. Yes, a good diet can make us feel healthier and more energetic. Yes, losing weight can give us the confidence to go on to achieve more. But these are by-products of a healthy diet, not the result of losing weight. The foods you eat or don't eat won't do this for you, in fact the best predictor for liking your body is not the size of it or even how attractive you are; no, the best predictor is how you value yourself – your self-esteem, and, trust me, I have never seen a menu with that on it . . .

Food Judges

On the evening I was invited to Amy's house for dinner she called to say she had to cancel because the detox diet her herbalist had put her on was making her sick and gassy, so she needed to rest and de-bloat. I wished her better and put the phone down, feeling a little confused. A few minutes later my mother called, saying that she and my father were coming into town to see a show and asking if I wanted to join them for dinner.

I said 'yes' and a couple of hours later I met them at a chic little restaurant in the West End. When I arrived I found them sitting at a corner table. My mother was rearranging the salt and pepper shakers in relation to the vase of dried flowers and my father was snapping a toothpick into small pieces. My mother, who's in her fifties and still very thin and fit ('You are what you eat,' she always says), always orders the same thing – salmon on a bed of something green. My father, also in his fifties, never seems to order what he wants – in fact, he never orders his own food. Instead, my mother orders for him while sharing his medical history with whatever random waiter happens to be serving us. 'Yes, now, no salt for Howard, we're watching our blood pressure. And make sure that you only use soya milk for his tea; we don't want another nasty stomach upset – he was on the loo for three days last time he ate dairy.' After Mum has horrified our server and silence has fallen on those tables in close enough proximity to hear us, she usually looks over at me, indicating that I should tell the waiter what I want. 'Oh, is it my turn to order? OK. Well, since I've been a good girl and stuck to my new sitcom diet all week, I think I can have a night off. Right, I think I'll start with one of those cute little pork pies – hold the salad – and then I'll have the fried chicken, topped with the four cheeses, the butter-cream glazed potatoes, a side order of cauliflower cheese and for dessert, the chocolate marzipan fondue for two with extra cream. Great, thanks . . . oh and waiter, another Diet Coke please.' For some reason it always infuriates my mother when she watches me order food in a restaurant, and because of this I find myself reverting to a stroppy teenager and doing things just to annoy her.

As we wait for our starters (two glasses of water and a pork pie) my mother brings up the topic of dieting with as much diplomacy *as an animal-rights activist at a fox-hunt. 'That new Dr Atkin's diet, now there's something all intelligent, ambitious, successful young women should be on.' I find myself getting that tense feeling in the pit of my stomach, I feel as if I'm being judged as a stupid, un-ambitious loser who can't control my life, just because I didn't order soggy fish. Part of me is furious with my mother but the other part of me believes her. By the time my pork pie arrives I'm in such a bad mood that I order a side of chips, glaring at my mother as I do. As I shovel the food into my mouth I feel as if I'm eating to spite her, and then it hits me . . . Almost every time I eat it's about dealing with an emotion, be it revenge or guilt or comfort. I rarely eat just because I'm hungry, I actually feel and express emotions through food. Deep in thought, I notice the waiter set down the plate of chips and hear my mother trying to excuse my eating habits by making up some story about some rare intestinal tract disorder. I tune out and seek comfort in the warm, soft yumminess of my chips.*

We judge each other by a lot of things in life – the way we speak, the way we dress, the people we date. These things give us clues about and insights into other people, and this is nowhere more true than in the way we eat. Because food is so emotionally loaded, we ascribe meaning to what and how we eat.

We reason that a person who monitors what they eat must have good self-control, or be disciplined in other aspects of their life, or perhaps that they're trying to control their weight. We reason that a person who tucks happily into a cheeseburger and fries must not care about their waistline – maybe they have high self-esteem, a fast metabolism, or perhaps they've given up caring about how they look. Of course what is being eaten is further complicated by what the eater looks like. If the person monitoring their food intake is very thin, we presume they might have an eating disorder, or perhaps that they're a fashion model; if the person scoffing the burger is overweight, we see them as greedy or lacking control. We judge the food that different cultures eat, we judge the food that different classes eat, and all the time what we're really doing is making a judgement about someone else that will have an impact on how we see ourselves. The core beliefs we hold about our body image affect the way we judge our own and other people's eating habits.

A core belief about needing to work hard to look good and be accepted by others will probably lead to a relationship with food that is underpinned with guilt. It will also lead to judgement of others and their eating habits based on the notion that only disciplined people have the correct relationship with food and everyone else is lazy. Therefore our core beliefs about our body image have a strong effect on our relationship with food.

The etiquette and politics of food always astonish me. From the snobbery of the arrogant waiter who can't believe that you actually want your fillet steak well-done to asking everyone else at your table if they're having a starter to make sure your order conforms to the rest of the diners', there is a whole repertoire of how we 'should' behave around food. And when you think about it, so many social situations involve food, that it's no wonder we feel pressured to eat or not eat certain dishes depending on where we are and who we are with. Can you imagine a girls' night in without tortilla chips and a dip with a few bottles of wine? Or a lads' night out without several pints of lager and bags of peanuts, then a trip to the curry-house?

On a date with a new man, most women won't order a whopping great steak, or a big, smelly vindaloo. We think that if we order a small salad we'll seem more attractive, more in control of our hunger, and more concerned about our appearance. Of course, the guy is far too engrossed in his smelly vindaloo or his juicy steak to notice, but we still imagine the opposite. Or else we've starved ourselves for three days beforehand and been to the gym every day. Far from appearing slim and attractive, we'll probably be feeling tired and dehydrated – not the best date-boosters.

When you think about it, the importance we attach to food is ridiculous: a man won't order a salad because it's a bit 'girly', and a woman won't order a kebab because it's a bit 'manly' – while chocolate has taken the place of sex! Come on, food is just food! We can't survive without it. It's a pleasure, but also an essential. Don't let it become more than that. Be the first date he's ever met who polished off three courses and then started on his, if that's what you feel like. Better yet, next time your mother or anyone else raises an eyebrow when you order a dessert offer them a spoon and tell them to taste where you're coming from.

His and Her Diets

When we think about struggling dieters, or chocoholics, more often than not we picture women. We automatically associate obsession with calorie counting and cutting back with the female of the species. But why? Men must worry about their weight and diet, too.

The main difference here is the way that men and women see food. Research has shown that a lot of men actually want to bulk up. While women want to be slender and delicate, men feel better if they take up more space. This means that they see food as a substance that will bring them closer to their body ideal, not as a poison that will drag them kicking and screaming away from it. They simply do not attach the same emotion to food that many women do.

What about overweight men? Research has shown that up to 75 per cent of men were unhappy with their body shape. Around half wanted to be bigger, and the others wanted to be smaller. These results contrast with similar research on women, almost all of whom wanted to be smaller. OK, so we've established that approximately half the men who are unhappy with their bodies want to lose weight too, so why don't we have a stereotype of men studying calories or buying endless miracle-promising diet books? Because when men want to lose weight, they don't diet. Research has shown that about 25 per cent of men have dieted at some point in their life, a tiny figure when compared to the 95 per cent of women who have dieted. Instead they try to lose weight through exercise. For men, health means being more muscular, rather than slimmer. Men associate strength with health, while women associate thinness with health. More often than not, men want to change their shape while women want to shrink.

Men's tendency to turn to exercise may also be because dieting is seen as a feminine preoccupation. More likely it is because men see their bodies more in terms of what they can do for them, rather than how they look. They appreciate their bodies in terms of functionality and prefer to use them to achieve a goal, in this case losing weight. Men and women have always used their bodies differently, since the days when being a man meant you were the one who grunted, stalked out of the cave, found a nice cow for dinner, dragged it back in and waited for it to reappear cooked medium rare, with a nice peppercorn sauce. Men have always had to use their bodies that little bit more. Whereas women have always been taught to ask not what their body can do for them but what it looks like. This means that when men embark on a quest to lose weight or change their body shape, they attach less emotional importance to it. Ultimately, if they slip up, and eat that profiterole, or miss a session at the gym, they feel it won't really matter because they're valued for a thousand other things, such as their earning capacity and the horsepower of their sports car.

Food doesn't become the enemy of the average man, they don't let it affect their moods, they don't feel guilty or happy because of it. They don't see it as the key to their body satisfaction. Most men would rather play a few rough games of football a week than embrace the Cabbage Soup diet. By nature men approach problems in a more practical way than women. If the car needs fixing, the woman will hunt for the manual in the attic, but the man will already be under the bonnet pulling out wires and pressing buttons. Women, in general, like to think their way out of a problem; men like to work their way out of it.

Foreign Food

I love Lupita. She's babysat for us and helped Mum with the cooking for as long as I can remember. She's about fifty-five, not very tall and sort of round and she has the biggest, warmest brown eyes I've ever seen. Lupita always smells yummy and is always trying to feed me. Somehow she seems to have avoided all the discussions on the perils of cholesterol and fat and still cooks like they did back in the 1950s.

Last weekend I was visiting my parents and Lupita was over helping my mum. By the time I got up there I was exhausted, the diet/Gandhi-like hunger strike had really started to take its toll and I just wanted to lie down. My mother opened the door, gave me a hug and said, 'Why, Sarah, I think you're losing weight! Good girl. Now, you need to be careful because your face is looking a little drawn. I'll book you in for a facial with Alice.' She made me turn around, pointed out that it would be better if I could lose weight specifically from my bum and thighs rather than all over and then pottered into the study to get Alice's number.

I dragged myself into the kitchen to get a glass of water and saw Lupita standing by the sink. She rushed over and hugged me, crushing my face into her chubby shoulder – it felt great to see her. She stood back, still holding onto my shoulders, and shook her head. 'Leetle one, why you so skinny? You look like a burrito without the filling. Come, I make big cow-meat stew that you like and you eat and then we make the pudding with the rice. You see all the colour come back to you cheeks in no time.'

I smiled and began to take off my coat but turned around quickly when I heard her gasp, 'Oh, my gootness, where is your bum? A woman needs nice round bum, you always have such lovely bum, and now I can't see where it is going to – queeckly, seet down and eat!' Part of me felt compelled to explain to Lupita the virtues of my diet and why being slim was so important but another part of me didn't want to contaminate her with the 'ideals' that had been shoved down my throat for so long, so instead I sat down and shoved her warm, wholesome 'cow-meat stew' down my throat and revelled at being back in her wonderful world for a while.

The way we view food and dieting varies from culture to culture. It seems ironic that we all chase after the 'ideal' body when everyone has such a different idea of what it is. As I mentioned in the last chapter, in developing countries, weight gain and a fuller figure are seen as positive, a bulwark against malnutrition. To a lesser extent, this is also true in many South American and Arab cultures. A woman shows her love for her family by providing them with rich, plentiful food. If she gains weight it is seen as a sign that she is being adequately cared for.

It's important to recognise that a stick-thin ideal is very much the dream of white, middle-class society.

These differing values are reflected in how and what we eat. For example, many cultures see food as a way of connecting with family. In patriarchal societies seating arrangements around the dinner table are important, the husband and father is usually at the head of the table, and the women do the cooking and serving. Food is prepared slowly, with care. It is seen as a symbol of love and nurturing. In cultures where time is more important than nutrition and taste, food is mass-produced by strangers, eaten quickly and usually alone. Cultural norms of eating, like body-image ideals, vary hugely. If we accept this, we can begin to see how fragile they are. So, if we decide to diet for anyone other than ourselves, we won't please anyone, because the person next to us has an entirely different view from us on what looks and tastes good.

Beware the False Cost of Dieting

Don't feel that your diet is worthless unless you're spending money. In October 1992, *Working Woman* magazine reported that, at any given time, 65 million Americans were dieting, and spending more than $30 billion – that's over

£20 billion – in the process. Ten years on, these figures have undoubtedly risen, with some weight loss companies reporting profits in excess of $85 million a year.

The people the weight-loss companies make the most money from are the bad dieters. If diets were simple, we'd all do one, and then wave goodbye to weight-loss companies. But we fail and try again, and that's where the money lies for the industry. Why do we keep pouring our hard-earned cash into their pockets? Because, as a society, we believe that the more you put into something, the more you get out of it. If we invest a little more, we gain a little more. We imagine that the more money we spend on books, exercise classes and special diet foods, the slimmer we will become. How many times have you caught yourself sighing at a picture of Jennifer Aniston, then reassuring yourself that, 'Yeah well, she's probably got a personal trainer, a dietician and a personal chef. If I had all her money I'd be skinny too.' We believe we deserve better results if we're putting more into the diet.

Here are some more of my favourite dieting myths:

It is Only Overeating that Causes People to be Fat

Most of us think that overeating is the only cause of weight problems. However, animal research suggests that there are more than fifty causes of excessive weight, including genetic, metabolic and environmental factors. While overeating may have contributed to weight gain, it is not necessary in order to maintain a higher weight level, once reached. In fact, several studies have confirmed that 'overweight' people do not eat more than those of average size.

Dieting Is All You Need to do to Lose Weight

By dieting we mean calorie restriction for the purpose of weight loss. In the last ten years researchers have looked critically at weight-loss results. They have found dismal results. Clinical studies show that within the first year up to 95 per cent of dieters regain the weight they initially lost, and many are heavier than when they started the diet. In the USA, the National Institute of Health discovered that the maximum weight loss for people using commercial weight-loss programmes was around 10 per cent. After the first year, two-thirds of participants regained weight. Within five years, virtually every participant regained the lost weight.

Everyone Can Be Slim If They Diet

A common myth perpetuated by the media is that everyone can be slim. This belief is increasingly being challenged by current research, which suggests that the body has a set level for the amount of fat it stores, and resists reduction or gain to a weight different from its norm. This theory suggests that weight is determined predominantly by genetics and early nutrition. So a woman whose natural weight is 210 pounds can be physically healthy but unable to maintain a lower weight. Likewise, a woman who is perceived as underweight at 110 pounds may be just as healthy but unable to gain weight.

For many of us, losing weight requires us to break the tie between our food and our emotions. It's far easier to make an economic investment in dieting than an emotional one, it's easier to hand over cash than to work out your motivation and goal and how you plan to achieve the latter. But if we rely on financial investment to achieve our lifestyle change, the results are likely to be disappointing. No amount of money will change how you feel about the contents of your fridge. Only you can do that. Keep this in mind when you're doing the weekly shop, the foods you need in order to drop a few pounds and become healthier don't necessarily come with the words 'light' or 'low-fat' plastered all over them. Take the power away from advertisers and food producers. If you play their game, you are more likely to lose, when you weigh up the colossal amount of money that is ploughed into trying to make us buy the junk food in the first place. You can buy every diet book, sign up to every exercise class, and buy all the 'diet' food you like – but the best diets require a lifestyle change, not a shopping trolley full of gimmicks.

When we approach dieting, like anything else related to our body image, we must be confident that we are doing it for the right reasons. Dieting for your mum, partner, or friends won't work. Dieting to achieve the dream car or Malibu beach house you've always dreamt of won't work. But if you turn your diet into a positive aim just to be a bit healthier, your chance of success will soar. Don't think of dieting as a long-haul journey of denial and deprivation. Think of it as a lifestyle change. And that doesn't mean that certain foods are blacklisted for the rest of your life. Diets won't work if they control you. If you're in charge, you're half-way to a healthier, happier you.

Food is so closely linked with body image because we feel it is the easiest way to change what we see in the mirror. We rationalise that what goes into our mouths comes out on our thighs, bellies and hips and consequently makes us feel bad about ourselves. So what better way to fix it than to censor what we eat?

By linking what we eat to how we feel about ourselves we reinforce negative core beliefs that centre on a conditional acceptance of who we are. Saying things like, 'I've been a good girl because I've only eaten one piece of toast for breakfast,' sends the direct message that we should only accept and like ourselves if we are restricting our natural instincts. And this is counterproductive. Our acceptance of who we are should be unconditional, not based on calorie intake or dress size. It is only when we can do this that we are able to value ourselves enough to eat more healthily and to lead a more positive lifestyle.

TAKE AWAYS

In this chapter we discovered that food will have as firm a hold over us as we let it. By eating when you are hungry and stopping when you are satisfied, you'll begin to distinguish emotional from physical hunger, and enough from too much. That's a huge step towards a more positive relationship with food and with your body.

TASK 1

Use table 1.2 below to learn how to listen to your body. Next time you get the munchies ask yourself if you're thinking about food because you're hungry or because you're bored or anxious. If it's the former then eat; if it's the latter, come up with a list of more effective ways to help you cope. Do this for at least three weeks – you'll find that you're becoming an expert at knowing when you're actually hungry. Use the example in table 1.1 as a guide.

TABLE 1.1 (Example)

Where are you and what time is it?	Describe the situation around you	Describe your feeling: is it hunger or something else?	How other than with food could you cope with your feelings?	Plan of action
At home, front room 8.30 p.m.	Watching TV alone, nothing good on	Feeling bored more than hungry – if I'm honest maybe a little lonely	Call a friend. Go out. Do something more fun than sitting in front of telly	Ring Jane and get the goss on her new beau, then have long bubble bath
At desk in office 11.45	Can't concentrate, stupid computer keeps crashing	Am definitely hungry and p***ed off at damn computer – low on energy too	Must have food and maybe a sledge-hammer to bash in computer	Eat something – and take five-minute break

TABLE 1.2

Where are you and what time is it?	Describe the situation around you	Describe your feeling: is it hunger or something else?	How other than with food could you cope with your feelings?	Plan of action

TASK 2

1. Complete this sentence focussing on all the plans you're putting off until you lose weight:

When I lose weight I will *go on holiday, buy a new winter coat, start going out with my friends more.*

2. Now take those plans and next to each write down whether you could achieve this at your current weight. For those things you can achieve, stop procrastinating! For those you think you can't, write down why, then take the time to question your justification.

My 'when I lose weight I will' list	Can I achieve these things now?	If yes, why am I procrastinating? If no, why not?	Do I believe my justifications, or are they just an easy excuse?	What is my plan?
Go on holiday with my friends	*Well, yes, but I'll feel silly in a bikini*	*I guess it's just easier not to go. I'm sure I won't enjoy myself if I do*	*I guess I keep making excuses. If I really made an effort I could probably have a good time*	*Start challenging my negative thoughts about going on holiday – maybe even start discussing it with friends*

In doing this, you'll be challenging the reasons behind why you want to lose weight, and separating weight loss from other aspirations. It's a good idea to reach for this list every time you find yourself thinking, When I lose weight I'll . . .

TASK 3

Develop a more positive relationship with food. Make a point of cooking at least three healthy but delicious meals each week for yourself, rather than relying on fast food. Keep this up for as long as you can – in fact, try to make it the habit of a lifetime.

Chapter Four

SHOPPING FOR YOUR BODY

*T*rudy and Antonio called me on Tuesday, excited about the fact that Antonio had slept with Fritz (a German catwalk choreographer) and consequently managed to get us tickets for London Fashion Week. The show was tomorrow and apparently it was going to be fabulous. Now instead of being excited, or at least indifferent, I was overcome with a sense of nauseating dread. The idea of being stuck in a giant white tent with a bunch of models who collectively weighed as much as I did when I was seven was not my idea of fun. (Especially since I decided to give up on the stupid sitcom diet that was making me feel ill.) I had visions of all the beautiful people looking at me in the way that they do that makes you feel like you're a completely different species. A fashion show was bound to be one of the prettiest, shallowest places on earth and so being on display, both as watched and watcher, would be inevitable.

I began to think about what I would wear. I needed to fit in and not be noticeable so it had to be black. Thankfully most of my wardrobe is black. While rummaging through the darkness of my black, loose-fitting clothes I came across a pretty lilac dress hiding in the back. I took it out and noticed I'd never taken off the price tag. I remembered buying it a couple of years ago for a colleague's garden party – I had spotted it in a new shop on the high street and had visions (my visions always tend to be in slow motion to the soundtrack of

Jerry McGuire) of walking into the party confidently as my lilac frock fluttered in the summer breeze, Pimm's in one hand, canapé in the other. Unfortunately it rained that day so I went in my black cords and striped polo-neck sweater instead and spent most of the party behind the crisps bowl, drinking lager and avoiding people.

I put the lilac dress back in its hiding place and closed the wardrobe door. If I was going to go to the fashion show I had to go shopping, one of my least favourite pastimes . . .

Shopping's a funny thing. One day we return home, collapse on the sofa, in a smiling stupor, with bags full of new goodies. The next we storm home empty-handed, feeling depressed, weepy, and, most of all, ugly.

We've all given up on a pair of trousers because the smaller size pinches a bit, and there is *no way* we're trying the next size up. 'I am not a size [insert own dreaded size here]!' we declare. The success or failure of a shopping trip can be decided by a piece of fabric. If Marks & Spencer comes up trumps and we feel great in the first top we try on, it sets us up for the day. But if that first top is a little tight, a black cloud appears that follows us from shop to shop, fitting room to fitting room. And there's always the possibility of what may be the scariest challenge ever to face mankind. They're a fact of life, and one of those things that, once faced with, you feel silly if you back out of: communal fitting rooms. Who invented *them*? The *devil*? They're like massive caverns of self-consciousness and embarrassment. How can you avoid staring at someone else's boobs or bum when everywhere you look there's a giant mirror giving you a close-up shot? And how are you supposed to forget about the cellulite on your backside when you can see it reflected back at you just over your left shoulder? And the worst thing is that if you can see it so can everyone else.

Any woman can spot in another the tell-tale signs of 'I'm a size twelve, so that's all I'm buying, whether it fits or not.' We can all identify the bulges that scream, 'Please release me! I need the next size up!' Or, even worse, 'The magazines say crop tops and hot-pants are in fashion this season, so that's what I'll wear!' There's something to be said for feeling comfortable in a get-up that would probably fit a small child, but not when it's worn at the cost of a healthy body image. And that's where the problem lies, although shopping can be enjoyable, it can also reinforce our negative core beliefs about our body image.

The reason why shopping can evoke emotions as diverse and extreme as elation and defeat is because its sole purpose is to focus on our appearance and adapt what we look like into what we want to look like. Remember, many of our insecurities about our body image stem from this discrepancy. So, when we pick up a blouse that makes our cleavage look as pert and perky as we've always dreamt, the discrepancy is minimised and we feel great. If it makes our breasts look like the ears of an ageing Dachshund then the discrepancy is widened and we feel awful. Shopping can trigger negative core beliefs about our appearance that remain dormant until we are forced to take a long look at ourselves in a mirror. Shopping is one of the major arenas in which our body insecurities are played out – but it doesn't have to be. Like food and dieting, shopping can be as pleasurable or painful as you allow it to be. All you need to do is examine your thoughts before you flick through the clothes hanging on the rails.

Shopping Partners

First things first. Before we go shopping we need to decide who to go with. Most of us would rather go with a friend than alone because we see shopping as a recreational activity but also because we need the reassurance of a sympathetic, yet honest voice. Picking a shopping companion is like picking a partner for life: they have to be truthful, considerate of your feelings, supportive and, above all, you must be able to trust them. These qualities do not sit easily with the two main flaws most women possess. The first is a tendency to be too tactful, and the second is an underlying jealousy of, or competition with, all other women. Not great ingredients for the perfect shopping expedition.

Armed with this knowledge, there are really only two people who are great to shop with. The first is your mother: love her or hate her, she's probably always honest with you – and of course you hate her for it, but deep down you know she's right. So, no matter how much we might resent them interfering with so many aspects of our life, mums make good shopping partners. So who else? you wonder. Who else makes a better shopping pal than the gaggle of girls who normally accompany you? Well, you do. Sometimes our own judgement, unclouded by the distraction of everyone else's, can be the most valuable. When you shop alone, you have time and space to really 'feel' an outfit and go with your own instincts. It is also a great opportunity to work on your body image. Sometimes we use clothes to define us, to tell other people who we are. Eventually we see ourselves only in terms of what the clothes say about us, and feel uncomfortable wearing anything different. It's as if our clothes start telling us who we should be, rather than us choosing clothes that reflect who we are. When you're shopping on your own you're more likely to pick up something that takes your fancy, even if it is a bit adventurous. This means that all the *shoulds* and *have-tos* that define your choices are coming from you, rather than being dictated by anyone else. And because of this you may find it easier to challenge them. For example, you may tell yourself, 'I know my friends always say I look better in trousers, but I love this knee-length skirt, even if it does reveal my skinny ankles.' By challenging the restrictive beliefs that have defined our wardrobe, we will also begin to challenge those that restrict us to a negative body image.

The Promise of Shopping

I was at my desk trying to come up with a viable excuse to get me out of the office and into Selfridges, but could only come up with my stock plea that I needed to go to the osteopath because my dodgy coccyx was acting up again. Juliette, my line manager, looked at me as if to say, 'I bet you don't know where your coccyx is or how to spell osteopath,' but grudgingly agreed that I could go.

On my way to catch the bus I called Antonio to see if he could meet me, but he said he was busy with a plumber – this vague statement was more than enough information so I hung up and speed-dialled Trudy, Sophie and a couple of other friends – all to no avail as they were either at work or skiving for their own reasons.

I arrived in Oxford Street and went into Selfridges. Its windows were filled with giant felt flowers and fabulous scenes of people in designer clothes living wonderful lives. I walked in, dodging the eight people dressed in black threatening me with perfume sprays and went up the escalator to the women's department. I watched women, mostly in pairs, analysing how fabrics fell, what they hid and what they showed off. It was funny watching how all the women, looking at themselves in the mirror, moved around checking every angle of their bodies, and went, either in defeat or triumph, back into the changing room, with their shopping partner providing all the moral support such expeditions require.

'Can I help you?' a chirpy voice said behind me.

'Um, I'm just looking,' I said, a little too defensively.

'OK,' she said politely. 'Let me know if you need anything,' then walked away to fix a brooch/fondle the breasts of one of the mannequins.

I walked around the different designer rooms, touching the clothes, all the time imagining what they would say about me. I could be a masculine yet feminine businesswoman in Armani, a sophisticated but slightly slutty princess in Versace or a virginal, slightly frumpy English rose in Laura Ashley. Although some of it was tempting, there was nothing I could actually see myself in at the fashion show. As I perused the different designs I realised I wasn't just buying a dress but trying to purchase a fantasy – some confidence and results – that was what the windows and the designers were trying to sell me. The funny thing was that because I felt so anxious about going to the fashion show, I was incapable of having that fantasy so none of the clothes I saw seemed right. Maybe, I thought to myself, it isn't clothes that give us confidence, but confidence that makes us feel good in our clothes . . . I walked out of the ladies' department and into the food hall to further ponder my thoughts.

When men shop it tends to go something like this: 'I need a new pair of trousers.' This brief thought will be followed by a quick trip to the shops, the selection of the item, and a swift, effortless purchase. Job done, trousers acquired and back in time for Saturday-afternoon football. When a woman shops, it is an entirely different routine, because women don't shop for a shirt or a pair of shoes, they shop for a scenario. We shop with an event in mind and, more often than not, we know exactly how we want it to unfold. For many women there are psychological and emotional aspects within the shopping experience that are simply absent in most men. There is evidence to suggest that women can go into a kind of semi-dream-like state when they shop, becoming absorbed in their quest for the perfect garment and imagining how they will feel when they wear it and how people will react to them when they do. No surprise then that research has shown that 65 per cent of men buy clothing they take into the fitting rooms, compared to only 25 per cent of women.

A woman will think, Well, I've got Emma's party on Saturday and my ex-boyfriend will be there. I want to show him how much I've moved on so I need some gorgeous new kitten heels. Or, When I'm on holiday I want to meet the perfect man so I need a really sexy bikini. She assumes that clothes will do the talking for her in these fantasy scenarios. We give clothes a voice. How many times have you heard women saying, 'I love this top – it says, "sexy but unavail-able."' Or 'Do you think these trousers say, "mumsy"?' Not only do we want our clothes to look beautiful, wash well and feel nice, we want them to *say* things. It can't just be a red jumper, it has to say, 'Feisty, but warm'. It can't just be a gypsy skirt, it has to say, 'Laid-back and at one with nature'. Women use clothes when they wish to be taken seriously in tough work situations, to seduce the men of their dreams, to fit in at mother-and-baby groups. We use clothes in the hope that they will get us the response we want from others – it might be respect, it might be sex, it may even be a message about our values. But what happens when we don't get the response we're looking for – if the sexy nightie goes unnoticed and he rolls over snoring, if the business suit doesn't stop another suit from asking us condescendingly to get him a coffee or if the other mums have decided that you aren't . . . well, mumsy enough? When this happens our confidence about the way we appear to others and consequently our self-esteem take a beating. We feel let down not by the clothes but by how we look and once again those negative thoughts about our appearance come swarming into our minds.

Women generally invest a lot of time and effort in their appearance – and research shows that the more you invest in your appearance the more susceptible you are to a poor body image. The reason for this is simple: more of your resources, both emotional and practical, are put into making the effort so if things don't work out you have more to lose. This is why we get so emotional over clothes shopping. For women, clothes are more than just a solution to nakedness: they're the key to the scenarios we imagine in our heads.

So What's Your Dress Size?

Since my expedition to Selfridges wasn't a success I decided to head for the high street. As I looked through the shop windows offering everything from half-priced shoes to fast food and hair transplants I spotted a store I liked. I walked in, avoided the salesgirl who was making a beeline for me, and after browsing around for a while *under a sign that read, New Autumn Collection, I saw a top I liked, it was black with small silver sequins on the bottom and the cuffs. I was going through the rail trying to find my size when I spotted one, right at the back. Funny how the bigger sizes are always right at the back. I picked it off the rail and almost jumped out of my skin when I heard James's voice behind me. 'Hi, Sarah, er, . . . I didn't mean to startle you.'*

'Er, hi,' I said, startled. He was wearing a baseball cap, white T-shirt, blue bomber jacket and jeans. His nose was a little pink from the cold and he looked sooo *cute.*

'That's a nice top.'

'Thanks,' I said, then realised that there was a giant orange sticker proclaiming my size printed on the hanger. I quickly put it behind my back. 'I'm not sure I'm getting it . . . It probably doesn't fit, haven't tried it on, probably need a much smaller size . . . Just in a hurry because it's London Fashion Week. My friend slept with Fritz so we have tickets . . .' As I ranted nervously he stared at me sympathetically, trying to follow my train of thought.

'Oh . . . Well, I just came in to get some new . . . um, shorts.'

My mind started racing as I imagined his fabulous legs in tight shorts, then I started thinking about his fabulous butt – but I managed to pull myself out of my X-rated fantasy world long enough to say, 'Great!'

He smiled again, said goodbye and walked away, which was a good thing since my arm was numb from hiding the top behind my back. I hoped he hadn't seen my size, and ran up to the nearest till to pay.

When the sales assistant asked if I wanted the hanger I shouted, 'No!' grabbed my bag and ran out of the shop.

The success or failure of a shopping expedition often depends on the mood we're in when we set off. Negative core beliefs are more likely to be activated when we're in a bad mood than when we're in a good one, we're more likely to explain what's going on around us in terms of already established, and often negative, core beliefs. On a good day, we'll squeeze out of the tiny bandeau top, throw it on the floor, giggle and think, This shop clearly only has clothes for prepubescent nymphs! No woman I know could squeeze into these tiny sizes! On a bad day, we'll drag ourselves out of the top, enter into the best sulk we can muster and moan, 'I am the fattest, most hideous creature ever to walk the earth. I will never be happy.' You see when we feel comfortable with our body image, we recognise that sizes from shop to shop are inconsistent, and that being a size bigger in one shop isn't the end of the world.

The reason sizes have become so important to women is because they have become the school reports that we and our friends judge ourselves by. Everyone knows that an A is better than a B. And, thanks to social conditioning, we have come to accept the idea that size small is better than medium, which, of course, is better than large. So a shopping trip is where we are assessed: have we failed or did we pass with flying colours? It's all down to the letter or number on the tag. You see, shopping should be about liking how something feels and looks, but unfortunately, more often than not, our negative thoughts that contain all the value judgements from the world around us sneak in and ruin the day.

The key to dealing with this is to forget about numbers – learn to ignore them. Forget the numbers your scales scream at you when you step on them. And forget the numbers on the labels in the back of clothes. We all know sizes vary from shop to shop, so why are we so distressed when we have to go for the next size up? If you're a size fourteen in one shop it doesn't mean you've gone up two sizes since that sandwich at lunch. Equally, fitting into a size eight in the next shop doesn't mean your metabolism has taken on the acceleration of a Formula One car and blessed you with the hips you always wanted. Don't get so wrapped up in the numbers. You're so much more than a number on a clothes label! And you have a choice. If you really can't face up to the next size, then by all means grab that too-small pair of jeans and huff, puff and squeal your way into them. But when you wear them, you'll always feel fatter than you are because they don't fit. Or you can reach for the pair that has a bigger size on the label, and every time you wear them you'll feel slimmer, as the material sits perfectly on your body. 'Going up a size' can actually make us feel better about our bodies.

Don't let yourself be judged by a number. The only numbers you should ever worry about on a shopping trip are those little digits on the price tag. And if they, ahem, slip your mind, then just remind yourself that you're refusing to be judged by numbers in clothes shops. You never know, it might work . . .

Evil Shop Assistants

Other people can have a negative effect on the way we feel when we're shopping too. And one in particular. You know who she is. She's there when you walk in. She looks you up, then down, then up, then down, lingering on your love handles for a little too long. Then up again. Then she forces the sides of her mouth into a strange U shape. You can't call it a smile – the top two-thirds of her face are devoid of emotion. Then she's off, back to the tills where she can talk about you to another one. Yes, it's the bitchy shop assistant.

They seem to have the ability to convey in a glance, 'You're too fat, too ugly and too poor to be in my shop. Get out.' And you try to ignore her, to get on with your browsing, telling yourself that you have every right to be there, and you will stick around long enough at least to look as if you're buying something. So eventually you grab something and head for the changing rooms. And she's there again! Or is it another one? Evil shop assistants all have the same manicured nails, upturned noses and size six figures so it's hard to tell. Anyway, this one takes the clothes from you, inspects the labels, catches sight of the size you have selected and has a private laugh, which isn't that private because you can see it on her face – and hear it when she tells the other girls. Even before you've tried anything on, you feel unattractive and self-conscious, and it's unlikely that a well-cut pair of suit trousers can do much about that.

However, there are four main things to bear in mind when faced with this situation. Dealing with nasty shop assistants is like riding a bike: it's tough at first, and you think you'll never get the hang of it, but once you do you'll wonder why you ever found it difficult.

1. Keep in mind your reason for being there. You want a new top, or to try on some trousers you saw in a magazine. You're not there to play punch bag to a rude shop assistant. So, focus on the job in hand and you'll probably forget about her. Shops are designed illogically, most want to suggest they attract a slim, stylish clientele, so you will find tiny sizes on the rails, while the larger, more realistic ones will be stashed at the back of the shop. You'll have to endure the 'shame' of asking for a larger size, but this is only an embarrassing scenario if you let it be. When you speak to the shop's employees, don't let them make you feel silly. Tell them exactly what you want, and how they can help you. Be polite, firm and clear. It's important to remember what they're there for.

2. Be able to laugh at situations. If you try on a camisole and it won't even stretch over your shoulders, don't stand there blushing, sweating, scared to ask for the next size. Make a joke about how silly it looked, or how ridiculous their sizes must be, or how you shouldn't have gone for the Anne of Green Gables look in the first place. In fact, say anything that doesn't leave you feeling awkward and uncomfortable. Any negativity you feel in this situation should be directed at the garment, not at yourself. In this way you'll avoid internalising this negativity and, thus, feeling bad about yourself. Once you show yourself to be friendly and relaxed, it will be hard for the shop assistant to maintain her disdain. And if she does? So what? It speaks volumes about her, not about you. In these situations there is often a power issue; by taking the initiative to be polite, friendly and laugh at an uncomfortable moment, you already hold the power. Don't let the 'next size up' be your Mount Everest, just laugh it off.

3. Don't let anyone tell you what you should or should not be wearing. If you are a slave to the words of a fashion magazine, your friends or a pushy sales assistant, you won't end up with clothes you feel happy about. Enjoy the shopping experience for what it is. It's not a chance to blindly follow the fashion trends of the moment, it's an opportunity to find clothes that make you feel good. Fashions come and go, but they're not all flattering. What's the point in buying an ultra-cool micro-mini if it makes you uncomfortable? Part of accepting your body is about wearing clothes you feel happy in. The clothes that look best will be the ones that make you feel the most confident.

4. Remember that you're not a mind reader – and that your core beliefs may make you see things that aren't there. Don't jump to conclusions about the sales assistant's behaviour. She may seem quiet because she's shy, or pushy because she's trying to show her boss that she's doing her job. Don't seek to explain her behaviour in terms of who you are but, rather, of who she is. By doing this you'll be much more objective about how she relates to you and more confident in dealing with her.

Making Fashion Work for You

When you shop, don't tear a picture of Jodie Kidd out of *Vogue* and pull it out in every shop as you try to achieve an exact copy of her look. Magazines are forever telling us how to 'get the look' or 'steal her style', but most of us aren't dressing Jodie Kidd. We're dressing ourselves, normal people with normal proportions, who don't necessarily look good in jodhpurs and a bra top. Don't feel you can't experiment – by all means fall in love with the hot look of the season, but adapt it to fit you.

Shop with a theme in mind. Say, 'I want to find a really sexy outfit,' or 'I want something really pretty and feminine.' Then you will find yourself shopping for you, not a shorter, fatter version of Jodie. Equally, if there's a look you feel comfortable with, don't feel you have to break free of it. Women may think they could write the shopping Bible, but in some cases we could learn from the boys. Men tend to find a look, then stick with it. It's why they have ten pairs of chinos exactly the same. Or sixteen blue shirts. There's a lot to be said for finding a style that makes you feel good and running with it. The fashion industry may try to teach us to change our look each season, but we won't feel good about ourselves if we need someone else to tell us how to look. If you feel best in a short skirt, then who cares if you own six hundred? It's far better than trying a new look that makes you feel dumpy and unattractive just because *Vogue* tells you you should.

Because our body image is connected with what we see in the mirror, trying on new clothes has the potential to make us feel either very good or very bad about ourselves. But, like everything to do with body image, this is within our control. Remember, first you perceive a situation, make sense of it, see how it relates to your core beliefs and only then do you have an emotional reaction to it. The reflection that looks back at us from the mirror may have to compete with the idealised notion of what we should look like, but by simply taking the time to question where that notion comes from and challenge ourselves on why we believe that the 'ideal' version will be so much happier than the 'real' one, we begin to take control of the core beliefs that make us feel unhappy with ourselves.

Hiding Behind Clothes

For many people clothes are a way to hide what we don't like about the way we look. When you feel bad about your appearance and expect negative social reactions because of it, then a logical course of action is to use what you wear as a defence. By hiding or correcting what you don't like with clothes, you protect yourself from being hurt. To some extent, this is a great idea. A push-up bra that gives instant cleavage or those knickers that seem to suck the fat off your tummy and deposit it on your backside will make you feel more confident about what you're wearing and what you look like. However, unless a balance is struck in how important such items become to you in terms of boosting your confidence there can be a downside. It's one thing to use clothes occasionally to enhance your appearance but quite another when they become a shield to protect you from the negative feelings you have about your body. A push-up bra and suck-it-in knickers worn once in a while are great, but if they are the first thing you put on every morning and you won't let anyone see you (or even look at yourself) without them, there's a problem. Because by doing this you're underlining the negative belief that (a) parts of you are so bad they need to be hidden or 'corrected'; and (b) you can only function happily in public, or even in private, when you look a certain way. Worse, if you never challenge these ideas by going into the public arena wearing something that doesn't conceal what you hate about your body you will continue, almost superstitiously, to believe you can only wear certain types of clothes.

This is another case where a solution becomes part of the problem. You are trying to avoid feeling bad about your appearance, but your self-protection is motivated more by trying to avoid discomfort than seeking pleasure. What this means in real-life terms is that you end up with a situation where you are rejecting what you look like, and eventually who you are, thus worsening your body image and lowering your self-esteem.

An interesting variation on this theme is a trend that has developed in recent years to do with designer-labelled clothing. A T-shirt is seen as rather bland unless it is plastered with a big Gucci or Prada signature. Designer clothes have become symbols of social standing, and research suggests that people who feel insecure or anxious about their bodies use designer logos and expensive labels as a way to divert attention from what they feel are their worst qualities. A middle-aged woman might hide behind a leopard-print Dolce and Gabbana smock because she feels attention will focus on her outrageous – and, most importantly, outrageously expensive – outfit. Or a young man who feels insecure about his love handles may spend thousands on expensive suits to deflect attention from his few extra pounds. Clever clothing and luxury items can make us feel great but only if, deep down, we feel good about ourselves already. By all means buy the clothes and the labels that make you look great, enjoy wearing them, but don't hide behind an amazing bra or a logo on your chest, in fact don't hide behind clothes full stop. Clothes aren't armour and even if they were it wouldn't help because when it comes to body image the enemy we have to battle against resides in our minds not on our bodies.

Fashion Conspiracy?

*F*riday 4.00 p.m. I'm waiting to get into the second day of London Fashion Week. Have talked about how I bumped into James on the high street for so long and in so much detail that now when I mention anything even remotely to do with him both Trudy and Antonio

plug their ears and start chanting, 'I can't hear you . . . I am deaf . . .'
so I've given up trying to talk to them and start eavesdropping on the
conversation that two women (one with hot pink hair wearing a black
coat and another with long brown hair dressed all in green) are having.

They seem to be engaged in a heated debate on whether or not
the rock-chick look will last another season. The pink one seems to
be arguing that because so many 'simple, everyday people' are
wearing it that it's not zuzzy enough (whatever that means) to be worn
by the fashionistas. The green one seems to have taken the moral
high ground and is arguing that because so many designers went for
the look last season they're duty-bound to have some influence of it
in their next collections because so many women will now be attached
to the look. At this point another one of them who I hadn't noticed
despite the fact that she's wearing a fur-lined canary-yellow parka,
joins in. She takes on a 'Martin Luther King I have a dream' tone and
starts to explain arrogantly that: 'Of course fashion needs to move
on, after all, if it didn't it wouldn't be fashion. People need designers
to tell them what to wear, to make them feel good about themselves
and tell them when they look bad, to show them what's beautiful and
what's ugly and, of course, to help compile what's-hot and what's-
not lists . . . They are our lighthouses in a sea of bad taste and cheap
fabrics. They give us things to aspire to and add meaning to our
dreary existence on this earth.' When she's finished speaking she stares
triumphantly into space for a minute, then adjusts the fur on her hood.

Trudy, Antonio and I look at each other in disbelief, then Trudy
sticks two fingers down her throat and makes a gagging noise and
Antonio and I burst out laughing. Thanks to the fashion canary, London
Fashion Week and even fashion itself isn't so daunting, after all. Like
most things, it's really just about how you look at it, and whether you
choose to accept other people's values or not . . . All I can say is,
thank God I don't see the world through a yellow fur-lined parka.

*

When you're wandering around a shopping mall or watching TV adverts, be aware of the pressures operating around you. It's not simply a case of liking a skirt and buying it. The system is more complicated than that. Somebody somewhere has sat in an office and decided that one look will be *the* hot look this season. It might be leggings. It might be chiffon. It might be 'tramp chic'. When you first see the supermodels flaunting the 'new look', you'll chortle at how ridiculous it is. But by the end of the season you'll have converted to the Church of the Lycra Leggings. Fedora hats now fill your wardrobe.

And the same people decide which body part is *the* body part of the season. The problem with this is that it's a little harder to choose these fashion accessories. Boobs, for example, don't respond to magazine fashion trends. So, you might have been the most stylish girl in your local when big, buxom, bountiful bosoms were spilling out of Victorian corsets all over Paris, Milan and New York, daahling, but now the look is subtle, discreet bees-stings, with cowl slashes to the waist. You can't do much about it. The push-up bra goes back in the drawer and you're browsing through plastic-surgery leaflets, wondering how long it would take to pay back the loan you'd have to take out for a breast reduction. Or mini-skirts suddenly flirt their way back into fashion. The six-foot-tall brigade, with their giraffe limbs, jump for joy while the other 90 per cent of us panic. The truth is, fashion does not focus on what our bodies are really like. They focus on telling us what our bodies *should* be like. For the fashion bosses, the money does not lie in the satisfactory body image of the nation's population. It lies in the insecurities and anxieties we feel when we look into the mirror. If we have problems, they can offer us solutions – at a price.

So, just as we've worked out exactly how to breathe with our new push-up bra on, and exactly how to work gangster chic in Tesco's, it all changes. We've styled our body for the look of the moment, and it isn't the look of the moment any more. So we find something else to be unhappy about. Suddenly the magazines, the TV experts, the adverts, the catwalks, the designers are telling us that boyish hips are in. We look down at our child-bearers and, yet again, feel dissatisfied. Remember, to some extent, it benefits the fashion industry if we feel unhappy with the way we look, so distance yourself and put things in proportion. It's far more important to find a style that makes you feel great than to adopt every whim that hits the catwalks.

In the same way that we have to learn to see through advertising for weight-loss products, we must appreciate that there is a conspiracy behind the way clothes are sold to us. In 1997 beauty chain the Body Shop launched 'Ruby', a Barbie doll with real proportions. Ruby's accompanying ad slogan was: 'There are three billion women in the world who don't look like supermodels, and only eight who do.'

The fact is that most of us don't look like the girls we see parading the latest fashions. Look at your friends, look at your family. They probably have hips. They probably have bottoms. They probably have boobs. Yet, time after time, we are told that the ideal we must aspire to is the body of an adolescent model. For years, the fashion industry has been very fond of using a masculine-style body to showcase clothes, so slim hips, flat chests and tiny bums have all been favourites of the fashionistas. The large number of gay men in the industry has often meant that more natural womanly curves have been passed over for the tall, slim, boyish ideal, so, from the word go, as the clothes tumble off the sewing machine and on to the runways, we are being sold an unrealistic image of how women look.

Interestingly, research shows that many women still include supermodels as role models, ahead of actresses, sportswomen and their friends. But they are also critical of the unrealistic body shapes used to sell fashion. Many women find the adverts for plus-size clothes hypocritical, because they show models who are far skinnier than their clientele.

Even though we recognise that the 'ideal' shape is unrealistic to most of us, we still attempt to conform to it. We know that Kate Moss's build is unusual, but we still long for it. We know deep down that a twenty-inch waist doesn't sit well with a forty-inch bust but we still like the idea. We still hope that, in the right clothes, we, too, can look like the supermodels. Distance yourself from those images when you're shopping. Don't aspire to be Kate Moss or Claudia Schiffer or anyone other than the sexiest, happiest 'you' that you can be.

Letting Go of Clothes

Because women attach such emotional value to clothes, they hold a special place in our hearts and memories. Even when the buttons are threatening to pop off and the skirts don't cover our backsides, they can make us feel young again. They bring back the memories of a first kiss, a first date, a first girls' night out, our twenty-first birthday, or just our wild, reckless youth. But as we grow and evolve physically and emotionally, we need to change how we present our bodies. It can be damaging to cling to years gone by if it is at the cost of accepting the person we are today. We might not be a size eight any more, but now we are valued for many things other than the size of our waist. By squeezing into the clothes you wore as a teenager, you devalue everything you have achieved. Keep the clothes, but keep them in your wardrobe and your memory. The person you are today requires an entirely different wardrobe from the 'you' of yesterday. It doesn't mean you have to be dowdy, or old-fashioned. It just means that dressing to turn back the hands of time will only make you feel worse about your body, because it won't work with you. You can keep the Lycra, keep the tube tops, but your body won't pay attention. It will keep changing, and only by accepting this can we really find the perfect way of shopping to suit our body.

Letting go of clothes metaphorically is important too. There is a lot to be said for how wonderful a favourite little black dress can make you feel and, believe me, I would not in a million years underestimate the euphoric high a new pair of shoes can bring – but it's important that we see clothes as a means of celebrating and enjoying our appearance rather than as a quick fix for our self-esteem issues. They are there to act as props to enhance our confidence or maybe even provide a bit of an optical illusion, but unless the person wearing the clothes already has the resources to value and like herself then no amount of clever dressing will do because everyone will be able to see right through it . . . it will be another case of the Emperor's new clothes.

Women and shopping have been tied together by cliché. There's the cliché about the woman who tries clothes on and demands, 'Does my bum look big in this?' There's the 'shopaholic' cliché. There's the cliché about the woman who lies to her husband about how much she spends on a shopping trip, and then hides the evidence in the bottom of the wardrobe. Likewise, men have a few shopping stereotypes of their own. The man who wears the same trousers for forty-two years, because there's nothing wrong with them, so why should he change them? The man who slumps at the changing room doors preparing stock responses of, 'Yes dear', and 'It looks lovely dear'. What's the big deal with clothes shopping? Nobody makes such a big deal about grocery shopping or picking out a new sofa.

That's because, as we've seen, shopping for clothes is linked so closely with the way we feel about ourselves. Good shopping makes us feel great. We love new clothes that make us feel sexy and attractive. Bad shopping, however, is a completely different kettle of fish. A bad shopping day can completely ruin our self-esteem and leave us hating the way we look. We expect too much from clothes. We want them to make our bum smaller, our boobs bigger and our stomach flatter. We want them to costume the dramas we rehearse in our heads. We do to clothes what we do to food. We give them too much responsibility. We blame them, we hate them, because it's easier than looking at the real problems – low self-esteem and a struggling body image.

Shopping should be a pleasure, a joy. So don't give it the power to distress you so much. If the shop assistant is a little snooty, then ignore her. If that size twelve is a little too tight, then laugh and blame the shop's shoddy sizing system. Or, even better, accept that the rough estimates that shops make as to what constitutes a size twelve, fourteen, sixteen or twenty are not a reflection on you. And refuse to be judged on the basis of your dress size.

Look at shopping for what it is. Don't let it be a chore. Don't shop to look like the latest pre-pubescent supermodel, shop for you. Start off by treating shopping as a job that needs to be done, and eventually you'll find out how easy it is to keep it in perspective. You need a new pair of jeans, you don't need to play doormat to a skinny sales assistant. You don't need to be bullied into the latest fashions. You don't need to buy a size ten to feel good. Keep your real motives in mind, and who knows you might even start to enjoy yourself.

TAKE AWAYS

Like most things to do with your body image the clothes you wear and the way you use them can have a profound impact on how good you feel about yourself. This chapter has shown the importance of not letting clothes, sizes or shopping dictate how you feel about your body. So, let's get down to some serious soul-searching and start clearing out our wardrobes.

TASK 1

1. Go through your wardrobe and find the items that you hide behind (maybe it's long shirts to hide your belly, trousers to hide your legs, or the platform heels that give you the height you long for). Lay them on your bed, take each piece of clothing in turn and make a list of the parts of your body you most frequently conceal.

Now put in order all the body parts from 'least dreaded' to 'most dreaded':

What parts of your body do you conceal or correct with clothes?

Example:

From what I can see from the six outfits on my bed I use clothes to hide my thighs, stomach, upper arms, hips and bum.

2. List in order your least dreaded to most dreaded body part based on the above.

Example:

My least dreaded body part is/are my: *Upper arms*

Followed by: *Stomach*

Followed by: *Thighs*

Followed by: *Hips*

Followed by: _____

Followed by: _____

My most dreaded body part is/are my: *Bum*

TASK 2

Beside each of the body parts you listed above write your worst fear if someone were to see it.

Example:

If someone was to see my   *upper arms*   they would think that *I was an absolutely disgusting person because they are so pale and skinny and untoned. They would probably call me a name or give me a dirty look.*

Ask yourself if it's a fair assumption to make that because someone has untoned upper arms they are a disgusting person. Examine the logic behind your statement. Do you really believe it? If you were to see someone's untoned arms would you think that about them? I'm guessing not, but for the sake of argument, let's say someone else does. What does it say about the person making the assumption? Not much! Now ask yourself in your adult life how often you have been called names or given dirty looks based on your upper arms. Again, I'm guessing probably never, but again for the sake of argument, let's say that someone was to call you a name: wouldn't it say a lot more about them than about you? Your assumptions are just that: assumptions. They are not based on hard evidence but on fear and anxiety. Even if, in your worst possible scenario, your fears are borne out, instead of taking to heart someone else's rudeness, see it for what it really is: a reflection of their own insecurities and fears.

Continue to do the same with each body part until you have challenged your worst fears about each.

TASK 3

Now that you have completed tasks 1 and 2 it's time for some relaxation and imagery. The technique described below shows us how to achieve Progressive Muscle Relaxation.

Progressive muscle relaxation

This technique was devised by Edmund Jacobson. The idea is systematically to tense and relax groups of muscles. Tighten each group and hold the tension for about five seconds, then relax for about thirty seconds. While doing this focus on the relaxation you feel in each set of muscles and enjoy it. You might want to record the following instructions on an audiotape so you can play them back while you lie down and close your eyes.

Close your eyes and rest for a minute. Let go of any thoughts or worries, tell yourself you can come back to them later, when your exercise is finished. Focus on your breathing. As you inhale give the air a calm, relaxing colour and imagine it entering your lungs, cleansing them of any anxiety and making you feel relaxed, safe and comfortable. Do this again, and remember to visualise yourself inhaling the calm, clean air and exhaling any stress or anxiety you may feel. Now we are going to turn to specific body parts. First, focus on your right hand and forearm. Make a fist, then release – note the difference between the tension and relaxation. Now move on to the right upper arm: bend the arm and 'show off your muscles', release . . . Focus on your left hand and forearm, make a fist, release . . . all the time noting the calm, relaxing breaths you are taking . . . Now the left upper arm: bend the arm and tighten the muscles, release . . . Now the face: begin with the forehead. Raise your eyebrows, relax your face . . . Eyes and cheeks, squeeze the eyes, relax . . . Now the mouth and jaw . . . clench your teeth and pull the corners of your mouth back, relax . . . Now to the shoulders and neck . . . Lock your fingers behind your neck and push back your head against this resistance . . . Pull up your shoulders and press your head back against their resistance (horizontally – not as you would when you look up), let your shoulders hang, relax . . . Now focus on your chest and back . . . Breathe in deeply and hold your breath, pressing your shoulders together at the back, then let your shoulders hang, breathe normally . . . Focus on your belly: tighten the abdominal muscles (or draw in the belly), release . . . Focus on your right thigh and stretch the right foot forward, release . . . Move down to the calf . . . Lift up the right heel (be careful not to cramp), release . . . Slowly down to the right foot . . . Crook the toes, release. Now move to the left thigh and stretch your left food forward, relax . . . Left calf, lift up the left heel, release . . . and, finally, left foot, crook the toes, relax. You have now tensed and relaxed every part of your body . . . Any remaining stress and anxiety is leaving your body as you exhale, and you feel calm, safe, relaxed and contented. Keep your eyes closed for a while and enjoy the feeling of calm and relaxation. Breathe in deeply and move your fingers and toes, breathe in deeply again and have a nice long stretch. When you are ready, open your eyes. The breathing and stretching will help you reactivate your circulation and refresh you.

Start the tape when you are relaxed, lying down with your eyes closed. Make sure you won't be interrupted – unplug any phones, turn off the TV.

Once you've completed the relaxation, imagine wearing an article of clothing that shows off a feature you normally conceal (if it's your upper arms imagine yourself wearing a dress with spaghetti straps). Now continue imagining yourself in it, all the time reminding yourself of how safe, relaxed, comfortable and positive you feel. Now imagine that people are looking at you, some smile, others come over to talk to you, but you are feeling safe, confident and happy. Now bring into the imagery your worst-case scenario – someone staring or saying something rude. Pay attention to what you are feeling and actively disregard any negative feelings – remember, negative comments from another person say more about them than they do about you. See yourself handling the situation comfortably, either ignoring the person or saying something that makes you feel better. Now see yourself walking around comfortably, happily – catch a glimpse of yourself in a full-length mirror as you walk by it and see yourself smiling and feeling positive. Tell yourself that you like who you are and that your upper arms, big or small, tanned or white, are a part of you. Slowly open your eyes.

You will probably need to do this twice a week for at least four weeks, or until you feel comfortable imagining all the body parts on your list. Remember, practice makes perfect: the more you practise your imagery and relaxation the better.

TASK 4

Now that you have conquered your negative thoughts with tasks 1–3 it's time to bring your success to the real world. I want you to live out the scenarios you've been imagining. Wear a garment that doesn't conceal you (start with the least stressful body part and move up). Make a date with yourself and do something simple, like going shopping in a top that doesn't cover your arms. Do this confidently – all that imagery and relaxation will have prepared you better than you think. Give yourself a specific task to do, such as buying some groceries. If you catch yourself feeling anxious, remember your deep breathing, relaxation and positive thoughts.

When you have finished go home and give yourself a huge pat on the back. You did it! You were in control of the clothes you wore and when you wore them, and you challenged the notion that you couldn't go out unless you were hiding behind them. Write down how your experience made you feel. If you felt uncomfortable about any part of it examine the thoughts behind those feelings and challenge them as in Task 1, until you can feel positive about the experience.

Now do the same for each of your other body parts, moving on to the next only when you have successfully completed the previous one. Eventually you will wear what you want not because it hides part of who you are but because that's what you want to wear.

Chapter Five
YOUR BODY, YOUR RELATIONSHIPS

*W*oke up late for work again, rolled over and realised that my face was wet because I'd been sleeping in a puddle of my own saliva. Wiped it dry with the back of my hand and sat up. Contemplated calling in sick and staying in to watch Trisha's exposé of a gang of pensioners who shoplift, but decided against it because remembered that today was the monthly interdepartmental meeting and gorgeous James would be there. Found a low-cut turquoise blouse that Aunt Cecilia sent me for my birthday last year and wore it with my long black skirt, which hides everything from the waist down. Got out my depressingly large pants – felt sad that there was little point in wearing anything prettier since unless I was in an awful accident there was no chance of anyone seeing them – tried to remember the last time when anyone had been near my pants and calculated that I hadn't been on a date, let alone in a position to show anyone my pants for almost a year. In fact, the last date I went on was a complete disaster. It went something like this . . .

My friend Sophie had set me up with a guy from her office – Jed. I was due to meet him at nine but I got there a little early so I could have some time to prepare myself. I remember feeling really un-comfortable because it was hot and my new G-string kept disap-pearing into my bum. After serious contemplation, decided to stand up and try to wedge out the fabric from in between my cheeks hoping no one would notice. However, as I slouched over the left side of the table, with my hand up my bum trying to wrench out the G-string that had by now travelled up to my appendix, I noticed someone walking towards me – of course, my prayers that it wasn't my blind date or that at least he might really be blind, weren't answered and he came over and said, 'Hi, are you Sarah?'

'Yes', I said apologetically, took my hand out of my bum and offered it to him. Then, of course, I realised what I was doing and took it away. He looked confused but we managed to smile at each other, sit down and both nervously look at our menus. I remember being sure that he was thinking what a giant blob I looked like. He seemed quite fit (teeth a bit on the big side and hair a little thinning but generally attractive).

'So, do you eat here often?' he asked.

I paused to wonder whether this was a quip about my weight but decided to give him the benefit of the doubt. 'I've never been here before.'

'Oh, well, I like the steak,' he said, and made a sort of grunting noise – trying to imitate a caveman, I think. It seems this was a sign of things to come because by the time we'd ordered he'd belched twice, talked about monster truck rallies for about twenty minutes, explained in detail the perils of athlete's foot and 'reassured' me that women with meat on their bones were a lot warmer to snuggle up to on a cold winter night.

When our waiter finally arrived with our food, I refrained from trying to stab myself with my fork and ate quickly so that I could get out of there. But, of course, it wasn't that simple. As I was about to swallow a large piece of steak he smacked my shoulder and said something about how nice it is to see a woman enjoying her food. This caused me to choke, so he got up, shouted to everyone else in the restaurant not to panic because he knew the 'Heineken' manoeuvre and rushed behind me.

Just as he was about to put his hands round my waist I coughed up the meat stuck in my throat and stood up. I thanked him and *told him that I really had to go. He offered to drive me – I declined. He asked for my number. I declined. He then asked if there was any chance of us spending the night together. I assured him there wasn't, picked up my coat and headed out the door. Before I left, he shouted, 'It's my nose, isn't it?' For a moment I had no idea what he was talking about until I realised he was pointing to a small bump on the top of his nose. I walked back to him. 'You're disgusted by the crook on the top, aren't you?'*

'No, I'm not.'

'Yes, you are.'

'No, I'm not.'

'Yes, you are.'

'OK, this is getting ridiculous – I'm leaving because you're rude, loud and have the table manners of a pot-bellied pig.'

'Really? Cool! For a second there I thought it was my nose crook that was putting you off.'

I smiled, happy that I'd 'reassured' him, and walked away, bewildered.

The funny thing about relationships is that we are drawn to them not just so that we can get to know other people but so that we can get to know *ourselves* better through their eyes. In fact, we are obsessed with reading other people's reactions to us, as if this will give us some insight into who we are but also as if it will help us value ourselves more effectively. Consequently, our body image becomes a key issue in the way we see and present ourselves in relationships.

We are always told, 'First impressions count.' Well, if we feel insecure about the way we look, that's not helpful because we feel as if we are already judged on the way we look before we've opened our mouths. Before a first date, we'll spend hours primping and preening because we want to create a good first impression. No, scratch that. We want to create a *mind-blowing* first impression, because thanks to the pop psychology we are bombarded with these days, we seem to think that first impressions are more important than all the later ones put together. This, of course, is simply not true. There is a lot of research to suggest that our interactions with people following a first impression are vital in developing the image they form of us. There is also strong evidence that we come to view people we like as increasingly good-looking the longer we know them. Likewise, even if we've decided that we like someone because of their appearance, this 'halo effect' will fade over time if the person's character doesn't meet our expectations. So, the idea that you get only one chance to make an impression is simply not true.

We live in a culture obsessed with image, and it's taught us to make judgements quicker than you can say 'superficial'. Some psychologists have compared us to actors who wake in the morning, put on 'a costume' and stage makeup. Then we go through the day 'in role', striving to present an image as real and true. Most of us are anxious about the way others will view us when they first meet us, we reason that if we apply enough makeup and make sure we've got the right costume on, we can create an image that will make us more acceptable to them.

Our core beliefs provide a basis for the new information we take in, and when we meet someone for the first time, we make certain assumptions, whether we are aware of it or not. For example, we may assume a man is rich because he has a tan. We may assume someone is childlike or vulnerable because they have a small frame. We tend to feel more drawn to those who appear most similar to us. Before we speak to someone, appearance is all we have to go on, so it's clear why someone who has a negative body image may feel uncomfortable in forming new relationships. What we have to realise, however, is that first impressions are fairly shallow.

The easiest way to challenge the beliefs that someone may hold about you from your appearance is to give them more information to go on. For example, if the assumption is that because you're short you will be childlike and fragile, you might want to talk about your recent holiday when you went solo white-water rafting. If the assumption is that you're deeply tanned all year round, so you must be rich and spoilt, you might want to mention that your Greek genes make it easy for you to tan and your work as a gardener (for extra cash to put yourself through college) means you spend a lot of time in the sun. Get the idea? We are programmed to make assumptions because that's how we make sense of the world around us.

However, we are also programmed to review and refine them with new information. The more information you provide about yourself, the more realistic other people's assumptions about you will become.

Strangers

O n my way to the office I found that my bra kept peeping over my plunging neckline and that I had to keep tugging up my blouse to hide it. This was fine at home, but when I got to the bus stop I realised that it looked like I was fondling myself and people were looking at me strangely. As I stood on the bus, holding the *handrail above my head, I became aware that a short, balding guy had positioned himself under my right boob and kept pretending to lose his balance so he could brush his shiny little head against me. I decided that although I liked my breasts I wasn't sure about becoming a masturbation aid for strangers on public transport.*

It was too late to go home and change so I held my work files over my cleavage as I walked down the road to my office building. When I arrived I noticed that people had already started to head for the fifth-floor conference room. I ducked into my office and applied some more lip-gloss from my juicy tube, wrenched up my top and made my way to the meeting.

When I walked in I spotted James immediately – he was sitting in the corner smoothing his hair and flicking his pen. The guy chairing the meeting explained that our company was doing the marketing for Diablo Bablo, a new drink that was being launched. It tasted like bubble gum, but had the alcohol content of a bottle of vodka in every glass. Bob, a really smarmy guy from PR, was addressing everyone. 'What we need to sell this,' he said, 'is an ass like Kylie's – you know, something that every woman wants and that every man wants to get his hands on.' Most of the women in the room (and, to his credit, James) rolled their eyes; most of the men giggled like little schoolboys.

At that point, as was customary in our very 'earth mother, we value every one's opinion' type company meetings, we were all invited to give our view on what had been presented. I was dying to tell Neanderthal Bob what I thought of his crappy drink and offensive ad campaign when I heard a little squeal from the back of the room. It was Suzy, the sparkly pink girl from the office party. She cleared her throat and said, 'I don't like Kylie's bum. It's too small. Um, I think J-Lo would be better. She's more womanly and, um, realer.'

The room fell silent and Bob smiled uncomfortably. 'Um, thanks for that. I guess the point is that we need to give people something to aspire to – I mean, let's be honest, who wouldn't want an ass like Kylie's?'

All of a sudden I heard myself say, 'Um . . . as far as I know Kylie is thirty-four, but her ass is about fourteen. My ass, on the other hand, has kept up with the rest of my body, so walking around in a silver mini-dress and sun visor is not something I aspire to.' All of a sudden the room was eerily quiet, and I could feel myself starting to blush. I didn't want it to seem as though I had a major issue with Kylie's or anyone else's ass for that matter, so I quickly added, 'I think you need something more relevant to the drink, you know, people having fun with it or enjoying the taste or something.'

Bob, who seemed utterly gob-smacked, thanked us for our comments and said the marketing team would take them on board. The meeting was adjourned, and I rushed out of there as quickly as I could for fear of bumping into James.

When we are feeling down or unsure, the appreciation or approval of others is far more important to us. It can be conveyed through anything from blatant flirting to a smile. Lack of interest can be conveyed just as easily. If the stranger with whom we have struck up a conversation at a party looks away from us, or glances at his watch, we will probably feel bad about ourselves. As we've seen in previous chapters, when we feel insecure, we often attribute negative interaction with others as a reflection of us, and if we have a poor body image it is focused on how we look. We may think, He's not listening, because he doesn't want to waste time speaking to me, because I'm not pretty enough. So, the way we behave towards him reflects this. We might try to avoid drawing attention to ourselves, or hesitate to make conversation for fear of rejection and come across as less confident, and more self-conscious – traits that don't make us attractive to others. If the same stranger smiled, nodded or flirted, our self-esteem may be dramatically boosted. If he chats us up, we may feel sexy, attractive and confident, which makes us appear even more attractive, so our positive thoughts feed into our behaviour and vice versa.

The problem is that we anticipate the reactions of others when we first meet them and these self-fulfilling prophecies are always a recipe for disaster. If we are having a bad day – you know, those ones when perhaps your hair's decided to take on a frazzled look that no amount of serum can tame, or those trousers feel a bit too tight, then we're more likely to assume, 'This person won't like me,' so we act in the way we think they expect us to. This will no doubt lead to the conclusion we were expecting, and so reinforce the negative beliefs we hold about our appearance.

In order to protect ourselves from being hurt in relationships we make sure not to give someone the chance to reject us, or put us down, so we shy away from conversation. We may even reach a point where we give up trying to endear ourselves to new people altogether, because we believe we'll always fail. 'Learned helplessness' is what psychologists call the process of simply giving up on trying to achieve something because we are so convinced that it will never happen. Not surprisingly, it tends to occur after we've experienced a series of failures. We become passive and depressed, and to cope with our negative feelings we struggle to accentuate the 'cause' of our failure so that it is easier to blame. So, for example, if we feel we have difficulties making friends because we are overweight, we may eventually give up trying to slim down or dress attractively, feeling that if we look as good as we can, yet *still* fail to succeed socially, then we will have to accept that we really are a failure. On the other hand, if we slob around in giant clothes, and refuse to lose weight, then we can blame the difficulties we have when meeting people on those things. It lets us off the hook a little bit, but by doing this we only confirm to ourselves that we don't deserve to feel good about ourselves or to like who we are. The only way forward is to take a chance – to stop using those harmful self-protection techniques. The only way forward is to confront your anxieties – by doing this you will be confronting head on those core beliefs that are restricting you from living your life to the full.

It's important for us to remember that most people have anxieties about meeting new people. Everybody wants to feel they are accepted and liked. It's just part of being human – and if we didn't care about the way others saw us, we'd have no place in society. Often people excuse the way they look before others have even had a chance to notice it. We all know a friend who always makes of point of acknowledging, or pointing out, that she isn't looking her best in the fear that if she doesn't someone else will – 'I know I look really tired and drawn today . . . etc., etc., etc.' We need to move away from defining ourselves as a body, good or bad. Imagine how little sense things would make if we judged everyone purely on the way they looked, only consulting doctors and scientists if they were attractive to us, voting for a politician with an atrocious human-rights record because she was the best-looking candidate, playing with children only if they were beautiful. It's a complete waste of time to judge and evaluate ourselves and anyone else in terms of the way we look, because our purpose and our value as human beings run so much deeper than that. It's important that we remember to see our bodies as tools that we can use to enhance our lives, to see them as functional more than aesthetic. Otherwise we might as well all just go and stand very still in a shop window, and wait for a shop assistant to dress us.

There is evidence to suggest that the more active we are, the healthier our body image will be, because it helps us put things into perspective. This is in fact true of both able-bodied and disabled people. The point is to be able to enjoy your body for what it can do rather than focusing on what it can't or on what it doesn't look like. This is one of the best ways to boost body image and self-esteem. Rather than thinking, My flabby arms are ruining my life! think, My arms enable me to be a really good tennis player! Appreciating our body for what it can do for us will serve to take away the focus from the false and damaging notion that the complete worth of our bodies lies in how they look.

Friends

We've established that in groups of strangers we may feel self-conscious, as we worry that they will judge us on the way we look, and that the first impression will be the lasting one. But how do we feel among friends and family? They know us on a much deeper level so surely we must feel more confident and relaxed, right? Not necessarily. An interesting idea called Social Comparison Theory suggests that we need accurate, truthful assessments of our personal qualities to feel good about ourselves. To do this we tend to compare ourselves with others. If we feel someone looks better than us, we make an upward comparison; if we feel we look better, we make a downward comparison. So, in any group of people, even those that we know, we are still likely to make upward comparisons, which cause us to feel bad about ourselves. For example, we might compare ourselves to our younger sister, and think, She's got much better boobs than me, or with a group of girlfriends, and think, I'm the fattest one of all my friends.

We are also conditioned to believe that a woman's desired goal in life is to find the perfect man to swing through the trees, bang on the cave door and bring home a wild boar for dinner (or something like that). So, other women become our rivals. But ultimately, of course, we're only really competing against ourselves. And we'll never win, because we're running a race with no finish line, or boxing with no opponent, or playing a game against the computer. Every slim, tall, willowy blonde has probably wished at some point that she was a petite, curvy brunette. Likewise, the curvy brunette has probably wished she looked like her blonde friend. We tend to focus on what we're not rather than focusing on the qualities we do possess. And this points us to the answer to the problem – it feels unnatural for many women to stare into a mirror and list the things they actually like about their bodies. But, like most things we hate doing, just like exercising, eating healthily, and colonic irrigation, it's very good for us. Why stand in front of a mirror putting yourself down when it makes you feel so much better, once you've got over the awkwardness, to praise your positive qualities? Makes sense when you think about it.

Dating League Tables

My cousin Beatrice is great. She's probably the one member of my family I actually like. Even though she's really successful and pretty (got a first from Uni and has naturally curly hair) she's still *really down-to-earth and nice (listens politely to Uncle Tom – even though he's senile and always rambling on about the engineering genius behind incontinence pants – and she volunteered for a year on an environmental farm in India). So when I received an invitation to her wedding (apart from almost having a heart attack because I had no one to go with) I was really chuffed – until my sister rang. She was talking in an excited breathy voice that disturbed me, she asked if I'd had the invitation and started giggling. I told her I had, added that she sounded weird and asked why she was laughing. 'I've seen him! The guy she's marrying!' she squealed, and began to describe Martin, who, according to my sister, left a lot to be desired in the looks department.*

While I listened to her describe him: short, no chin, pudgy, drives a mediocre car, I realised I was detecting an air of triumph in her voice. When I asked her about it, she started talking in this hushed whisper and said, 'Don't you get it? She's not so perfect after all . . . I mean if he's the best she can do for a husband . . .'

Now, I have to admit that even though I was aware that my sister was not the deepest, most sensitive person in the world, I'd never expected her to sound like such a small-minded witch. I was, in fact, deeply offended that she could judge this guy on looks alone, and also see it as some sort of weakness or personality flaw in Beatrice that she could go for him.

I put the phone down and was aware of the football results being read out on the TV in the background – and all of a sudden it dawned on me that league tables were what my sister had been talking about. Beatrice, clearly a Premiership leader Man U type, was marrying Martin, a Tranmere Rovers third-division loser. So what was I, then? What did my sister and the rest of the world see me as? Was I ridiculous for pining after James (who is at least a Chelsea if not an Arsenal)? Would he think I was out of my league and laugh at me? Most importantly, who did I see myself as? I picked up the

phone ready to call my sister and tell her what I thought of her and
her stupid shallow beliefs, to tell her that Martin and I could date in
any league we wanted to and that Beatrice was probably very lucky
to have him . . . but then it occurred to me that, really, I was no
different from my sister. I, too, had looked at people in the street and
wondered what they were doing together – worse still, I had always
made sure to go for guys like me – average. Even when I was younger
and into boy bands I would never dream of going for the cutest one,
somehow I felt I wasn't allowed to like him and needed to show alle-
giance to the guy with the weight problem – but the good voice and
musical talent – that none of the other girls liked. The only exception
has been James, whom I've had a crush on for months, but then
again I won't do anything about it because . . . he's not in my league.

I slumped in front of the TV, depressed and defeated. I reached
for my half-eaten Mars bar, but as a sign of defiance I put it down,
stood up and walked over to Gary Lineker who was talking excitedly
about a free kick. I pointed at him and promised myself, out loud,
that I would not be defined by a league, I would not be like my sister,
and that I would speak to James . . . maybe even invite him to come
with me to Beatrice's wedding . . .

We worry about what other people will say about the match
between us and our partner. Lots of women go through
the following scenario.

Finally, after months of eyelash-fluttering, and photo-
copier-lingering, the hot guy from Accounts has asked you
to have dinner with him. Rejoice! You ring your friends and
give them a blow-by-blow account of how he asked, covering
every tonal change in his voice, and exactly how many times
he smiled during the conversation. You even ring your
mother, and warn her that perhaps she needs to start
looking in Mothercare, and preparing for an obviously

imminent marriage and new arrival. But then it hits you: if he's so great, maybe he's too good for you. What were you thinking agreeing to go out with him? And then, the old favourite: 'He's out of my league!' Of course he hasn't noticed, or doesn't care about, your short legs or small chest, but now it's all you can think about. And even if he hasn't noticed, you convince yourself that he will, once he catches the stares of strangers in the restaurant who are thinking, 'What the hell is he doing with her?' Social-matching theory tells us that people often attract and end up with those who are similar in terms of attractiveness to them. So we assume that fantastically good-looking people will form relationships with other people who are fantastically good-looking. So, perhaps you turn up at the restaurant and act nonchalant and aloof, thinking that at least if he realises your aesthetic inequalities, you can say *you* rejected *him*. Usually, your first date rapidly turns into the last, and you're back at square one.

The saddest thing about this scenario is that the poor guy has absolutely no idea that these complex and irrational games are going on in your head. The friendly, warm, funny lady that he used to hang around the photocopier for has suddenly turned into the ice witch. And the joke of it is, that the whole time you were convincing yourself that your flabby tummy would be the cause of this relationship demise, he's just been sat there worrying about how attractive you are and whether you've noticed that he has droopy shoulders. He may look perfect to you, but he's got body anxieties too.

The body pressures we place upon ourselves when approaching new relationships relate to what we think the opposite sex finds attractive. Women believe they must be slim and busty because that's what every man wants. And men think they have to be big and bulky, because, of course, that's what women want. However, more often than not, our predictions are wrong. We strive for an ideal that we assume exists – and we have no idea what it is! In a recent study 500 men and women were interviewed on preferred body shapes and sizes for themselves and their partners. Results indicated that neither sex could estimate what the other would find desirable. The men guessed that the women would choose a bigger figure than they did, and the women guessed that the men would choose a smaller one than they did. Other research has supported these findings.

The best way to deal with first-date nerves – and meeting strangers – is to do whatever it takes to make you feel comfortable. Tell your favourite summer holiday anecdote for the hundredth time if it always gets you a laugh. So what if you always wear that red, beaded top? If that's what you feel best in, it's what you should wear. If it means having an expensive manicure the day before, then go ahead. Be the version of you that you like best. If that's the 'you' with a new haircut, kitten heels and a pencil skirt, then so be it. Two things are important to remember in these situations:

1. You only see yourself as you do because you've been with your body since the beginning. We've talked about how core beliefs stick with us even after our appearance changes so we might look into a mirror and still see that fat, bullied schoolkid. Or we might remember the hurtful words of a former partner. But a new person takes us at face value. They don't know about all the other stuff that you've been through. You look at your body through years of experience. They look at your body and like it for what it is now.

2. No one is immune from body anxieties. We all grow up in the same society and, to some extent, we are all seeking approval. We all want to be accepted, and we all worry that we won't be. Put your concerns into perspective. Appreciate that your date will probably feel like you do. Concentrate on putting them at ease and making them feel good, and your own anxieties will seem easier to cope with.

After the Kiss Goodnight

*A*ntonio rang on Thursday night. When I picked up the phone all I could hear was some snivelling and a high-pitched sighing. Finally, he said, in a voice so full of drama it would have made Liza Minnelli seem understated, 'Neil didn't call.' I wondered what had happened to Fritz already but didn't bother asking since Antonio's relationships were not generally renowned for their longevity.

'That's right . . . he said he'd call but he didn't. I know it was just one date but I'm certain he was my soulmate.' He stopped for effect and then continued. 'He specifically said when we kissed goodnight that he'd call, he smiled like this,' (again, we were on the phone so I'm not sure what Antonio was doing) . . . 'and said "Antonio, I will call you" . . . and that was eight days ago! Why, Sarah? Why? Why? Why? Why? Why? What's wrong with me? Am I so unlovable? It's my overbite, isn't it? It doesn't really make me look like Freddie Mercury, it makes me look like Prince Charles. Oh God! I'll never be loved again, or worse yet I'll never have sex again . . .'

In between cursing an orthodontist named Ed and declaring self-inflicted celibacy, I managed to get his attention and calmed him down a bit. I tried to make him feel better by insisting it was Neil's loss and that I was sure another soulmate was just round the corner, but he seemed convinced that his overbite had driven

Neil away – and was, in fact, responsible for all the relationship traumas he'd ever had.

Listening to Antonio talk, I realised that rejection was part of life and certainly a big part of dating. I also realised that one of the hardest things to deal with is that grey area between rejection and limbo – when someone says he's going to call and then doesn't, leaving you to speculate as to which of your personality or physical flaws have driven him away.

I tried to reassure Antonio about his teeth but he wasn't having it. Eventually, he blew me a kiss and said that he was going to spend the night in with Ben and Jerry (two men who always made him feel good no matter what) and that he would call tomorrow. As I put the phone down, I felt I'd let Antonio down – he clearly needed to feel lovable and gorgeous and I hadn't helped him. I wondered if we all looked to what we hated about ourselves to explain what other people hated within us – God knows, there have been times when I've blamed the size of my bum for everything from men not calling to the guy at the video shop giving me the wrong DVD. So maybe there was something to be said about the way that we make sense of things – or no sense at all – for that matter.

I picked up the photo of Antonio, Trudy and me from my dresser. We were at Disneyland Paris, wearing mouse ears and pulling silly faces. I gave him a kiss on the cheek and told him that he was my gorgeous fabulous friend, no matter what he thought, I closed my eyes and tried to think happy thoughts about my bum.

So, let's fast forward a little. From your point of view, your date went well. The conversation flowed, he laughed at your anecdotes, and you ended the night on a kiss that lingered too long to be called friendly. You went home sure of a follow-up date. Now a week has gone by with no phone call, no email, no flowers, not even a tacky little text message. What did you do wrong? You didn't talk about past relationships, you offered to pay half the bill, and you definitely checked your teeth for straggling spinach before the kiss. And then it hits you: it must have been the spots on your forehead. There's no other explanation. Just as you'd managed to banish your spotty-skin fears, they come back to haunt you. You start kicking yourself for having thought you could hide them from him.

This is a common date-failure thought process. If we can't see any other reason for lack of interest in us, we automatically blame the things we feel most insecure about. If you find yourself in this scenario, the first step in putting the situation into perspective, and salvaging your confidence, is to acknowledge that there are a million and one reasons that could explain the absence of a phone call. He may have lost your number, he may have thought you weren't interested and given up. He might have been looking for a one-night stand that you didn't offer. There are thousands of alternative explanations that are a hundred times more likely than his disgust at your pimples, or her repulsion at your bald patch. It's not reality that hands us the pimply-forehead explanation, we choose to use it because it fits our insecurities. And, anyway, suppose your date rejected you on the basis of something as ridiculous as your thinning hair or spots? What are you losing? Someone who values appearance over everything else. Which is not much of a loss when you think about it.

Sometimes after the kiss goodnight we realise we've kissed a frog but try to convince ourselves that he's a prince for fear of losing his affection – affection that we convince ourselves we need to boost our self-esteem. If we don't have the confidence to take a few risks, we can find ourselves settling for what we can get, because that's all we think we deserve. This is especially true of the aspirations we have for the type of relationship we hope to find. If we've always felt like the plain girl who will be left 'on the shelf', then it's quite hard to have any great hopes of finding the perfect partner. For a start, we try to fit ourselves into the boxes that society 'helpfully' creates for us. So if at school we were the stereotypical plain Jane who the boys thought was funny, but totally undesirable, it's hard to crack that mould. If you're used to being described as 'a good laugh' when really, you'd much rather be 'beautiful' or 'sexy', then it's hard to feel like anything else. It sets a standard for the way we behave around men. We don't present ourselves as sexy, confident and attractive because we've never felt like that. We approach every guy as if he was 'a mate', not as a 'mating partner', but as in 'oi, mate!'.

Years on, we still remember what it was like to get over-excited about the company of a boy we were totally in love with, only to realise that he was trying to get closer to our best friend. Or perhaps you were the boy that none of the girls fancied at school, so rather than waste your time talking to them you concentrated on terrorising them instead. If a girl received a short, sharp blow from a foot-ball to the back of the head, it was you who kicked it. If a girl found a frog in her bag, it was your doing. Years later, you find it hard to accept that the women around you now, perhaps the girls at work, aren't going to reject you in the same way as the school girls. And if they do, at least you'll have learnt that putting frogs in bags isn't the best way to deal with this. Hopefully.

We will always have social stereotypes, but there's no reason for you to assume one. It's up to you to break free from it and aspire to more than it allows you. If you play the part of the plain girl, you won't give the real 'you' a chance. Don't be defined by your appearance. Don't make it easy for people to look at your size and make assumptions about your personality and your lifestyle. Refuse to be what people might expect. You'll achieve far more than you probably imagine you deserve.

The Emperor's New G-String

Most of us have an exaggerated opinion of the effectiveness of Lycra and clever stitching to make us look better. Even though what you wear can make you look better or worse, it won't drastically change the way you appear to others. When someone compliments our figure how often do we reply, 'Oh, God, no! You should see me naked!' But if other people think we look good, it's probably because we *do* look good, not because our favourite high street shop has performed a mini-miracle. But, of course, we don't see it like that.

The fear of being 'found out' often happens at the start of a new relationship. We've had a wonderful few dates with a great guy and the moment of truth arrives – but we're so scared he'll think us a fraud when he finds out it's our Wonderbra, not our natural breasts, that makes us look so perky that we avoid showing him our body. How shallow do we think men are? Can you imagine enjoying someone's company, finding him attractive, fun to be with and a good catch, then getting into bed with him, noticing a couple of spots on his back and getting straight out? Of course not. So why should a little cellulite matter to him?

Most men don't even know what it is. And if yours does it's probably only because you've made him stand there and watch you pinch the skin on the side of your leg and pointed out in detail the dimples it makes.

If people want to have a relationship with you, it's because they've fallen for the whole package, not because they think that underneath those baggy clothes you're hiding the body of a supermodel. If you think you've carefully disguised those slightly flabby arms, and getting naked would entirely spoil the illusion, you're probably wrong. Either he has noticed them, and he doesn't care, or he actually finds you attractive, despite your own beliefs about yourself. Or perhaps you have succeeded with the upper arm concealment, but, let's face it, as soon as he does get those 'bingo-wings' out in the open, he's not likely to notice them anyway. Sometimes we credit men with far greater attention to detail than is realistic. If you don't believe me, listen to a group of men describing someone. It'll go something like this: 'Brown hair, I think . . . short . . . wearing a suit, or at least a jacket, I think. Beard – er, maybe.' It will not go something like this: 'Nice front teeth, split ends, relatively clear skin on forehead, knobbly knees.' As with all aspects of body dissatisfaction, the things that seem overwhelmingly important to us, often go completely unnoticed by other people.

Intimate Relationships

Feeling insecure or unhappy with the way we look can make us do pretty ridiculous things. It can make us talk endlessly about 'repulsive' parts of us that no one else notices. It can make us question whether we will ever find that special someone. And when we do, just as things start getting intimate, it can make us hurl ourselves towards the light switch so that that special someone won't discover 'the truth'. We spend so much time obsessing about what we hate about ourselves that when the time comes for someone else to see our dreaded (insert own most hated feature) we convince ourselves that our partner simply won't cope with the vision he'll be confronted with. So what do we do? Well, to save us and them the embarrassment, we evolve hide-and-disguise behaviours that would make any undercover agent proud.

It's like an automatic reflex in some women: as soon as his hands wander towards a zip or a button, we develop the reaction speed of a top-class sprinter. Off goes the light, removing any chance of him spying any flesh that might give the game away. And afterwards? Our body worries can force us to believe that sliding along the bed, desperately clutching the sheet to us is a foolproof move. Those lightning-quick fingers help us scramble into discarded clothes on the floor. Next time, we think, I'll make sure I throw my dress sexily just beside the bed so I can get to it quickly. And then, the greatest challenge – how to cross the treacherous gulf between the bed and the bathroom without him seeing how horrible we look naked. We duck, dive and camouflage until we reach safety. No wonder we all like dinner dates so much, we need all that food for the energy to get round the bedroom obstacle course.

For most of us coming to terms with our bodies is a major hurdle. It is not easy to accept that being sexy is not synonymous with being a size eight. We battle against our negative thoughts, trying to be more positive about how we look. And just as we've stopped staring at ourselves critically in the mirror, we're confronted with something even more terrifying: letting someone else stare at us naked. Self-acceptance is one thing, but most of us need others to make us feel truly acceptable. This is because we're not wired to be alone in the world but to live and function within groups. As a consequence of that, the norms and opinions of these groups are bound to be important to us. And I know we've said this before, but it's so important that it bears repeating: the core beliefs that make up a blueprint for how we interpret our world are always sensitive to the views and perceptions of others.

For most of us clothes are a physical *and* mental barrier that allows us to feel more secure and comfortable. When they come off, and the real thing is standing there in all its glory, we wonder if the other person is focusing on the parts of our body that we hate (or, worse, comparing us with others). We feel more naked than we've ever felt in our lives because we can't possibly be 'acceptable' as we are. Now, this will inevitably affect not only how we feel about ourselves but how we react to the person watching us. We hide, seek reassurance or laugh nervously. We are so obsessed with our own feelings we forget that the naked person across from us is feeling as vulnerable as we are. When we are at our most insecure we are also at our most self-obsessed – we fail to recognise that our reality may be different from other people's.

And this insecurity isn't just the domain of women, men can be just as bad. A major reason for this, of course, is the way men relate to each other. At least most women have the tact to avoid nicknames related specifically to parts of the body – 'Julie Five-Bellies', for example doesn't exactly have a good ring to it. But teasing one another about the way they look is part of everyday life for most men. And although the majority will laugh along at themselves so as to appear cool, if a guy really feels insecure about something, then this manly banter will only serve to highlight the problem. And when they're with the boys they might laugh about it, but every man can remember tensing to the point of oxygen-deficiency when it comes to getting naked with a woman. Look under any man's bed (try to avoid the other dangers that lurk there), and you're guaranteed to find at least one piece of exercise equipment, whether it be a set of free weights or an entire mini-gym. Let there be no doubt, men worry about how their bodies will rate when they are getting intimate too.

Just as women have role models, so too do men. Just as women think their men are expecting Angelina Jolie in the bedroom, men assume that their girlfriends are expecting David Beckham or Brad Pitt. The body ideal that men and women aspire to may be different but the basic insecurities are the same. And body insecurities can interfere with man's other greatest worry: his sexual prowess. While women may tense up in the bedroom if they feel anxious about how they look, men can encounter sexual difficulties. If you don't feel particularly sexy, it can be hard to perform. And as men are often expected to call the shots in the bedroom, this can cause massive insecurities. It's so ironic, the whole point of wanting to look sexy is that you will hopefully have a partner, but if you are obsessed with the way you look you might not actually be able to have sex even if you get the chance! Kind of defeats the purpose really, doesn't it?

Let's Talk About Sex, Baby

Contrary to every movie you've ever watched sex isn't like walking the catwalk at a Milan fashion show. Maybe Demi

Moore and Sharon Stone can look flawless while they're rolling, writhing and grunting, but that's with expertly applied lighting, makeup, and a director screaming, 'Demi, push your left boob to the right!' or, 'Sharon, put your left ankle behind your neck, please.' Sometimes it can be easy to forget that the way sex looks isn't important – the way it feels *is*. A flick through most women's magazines will reveal endless articles promising to reveal the 'Top Ten Most Flattering Sex Positions'. Very useful. You, too, can have pretty, elegant sex just like they do in the movies. But chances are, you'll have to fake the screams of ecstasy, just like they do in the movies. Because the positions that promise to make your bum look smallest and your tummy look flattest do not focus on what actually feels best. Referring to a women's magazine sex guide every two seconds, to check you're both in position, does not make for the lovemaking experience of your life. Forget about what sex looks like. It is, literally, one of those things that can be done with your eyes closed.

Also, sex doesn't discriminate on the basis of size and shape. And increasingly, neither do retailers. So, if you want to have fun with lingerie, go for it. Whatever makes you feel sexier can only be a good thing because you will feel more confident. If you love the way your boobs look in a really pretty push-up bra, then buy one. Don't become wrapped up in 'dressing up' for sex, becoming embroiled in the aesthetics of the business. But do whatever you need to do to make yourself feel sexier.

If you're panicking about something, talk to your partner about it. Sometimes we need someone else to laugh at our fears for us to grasp how silly they are. If you're planning to writhe around naked with someone, you should feel comfortable saying, 'I've always really hated my small boobs!' Sex is a noisy, messy business, and a conversation about body anxieties is one of the least embarrassing things that can happen. When your partner realises you're happy to talk about your concerns, they'll open up to you: 'What? I think they're great! I know how you feel, though, I'm always conscious about my appendix scar.' Suddenly the two of you can laugh about your – probably unfounded – body worries, rather than having a tense monologue in your heads.

To enjoy sex, you should feel that you can deal with whatever happens, and laugh about it with your partner, not dread their reaction. A significant proportion of women feel that their sexual relationships have suffered because of their body insecurities. These same women acknowledge that their insecurities have not come from their partners, who see them as attractive and are often oblivious to their 'flaws'. This explains why the partner lying next to you seems bewildered when you try to force their attention to your flabby belly or droopy boobs. 'I've put on loads of weight recently. You probably think I'm really fat,' we whinge. And the response they give will be wrong. It doesn't matter what it is, it will still be wrong. If your bed companion (who probably doesn't know what the hell you are talking about, and just wants to get some sleep) disagrees with you, they risk opening a whole new can of worms. That can go something like this: 'You're only saying that to make me feel better.' It's hard to wangle your way out of that one. If they agree that you're fat, but say, 'It doesn't matter, I love you anyway,' or 'I think you look better with a bit of flab,' you may have won the argument, but you still won't be happy.

Why do we go through this routine? First, we're seeking reassurance. A woman may feel awful about her spotty back, and needs to hear someone say it doesn't matter, even if she ignores them. Second, we all fear someone else noticing a problem with our appearance and thinking we're oblivious to it. Just as we flick through a magazine and exclaim, 'Doesn't she realise how stupid she looks?' we don't want someone (especially a bed partner) to be looking at us and thinking, Doesn't she realise how fat she looks? We want to call a spade a spade before he does. We assume he's noticed the square centimetre of cellulite on our elbow and want to make sure he knows that we know it's there. But remember, if this person has gone to bed with you, they find you attractive so they probably won't have noticed the thing you keep going on about. If they have, they certainly don't find it as repulsive as you do and, more importantly, will not see it as the most salient part of your body. So stop trying to make them! Constantly referring to your body worries is a sure-fire way to make you feel ten times worse about them.

The power to target and demolish our body worries comes from within us. Even if they were put there by other people, they cannot be taken away by other people. We have to do it ourselves. But it helps to realise that the reflection we see in the mirror is often far removed from the image our partners see. And the way we can help ourselves to understand this is to keep talking about it with our partners, in an honest and positive way. Remember, constantly pointing out your cellulite isn't helpful but being honest about your anxieties and feelings is.

Women and men have been rolling around naked together since the beginning of time. Sex is an essential function of life – like breathing, sleeping and eating. So, look at it in that way. Don't build it up to be the mystical magical performance you see on the silver screen. If you do, you will feel you're not beautiful enough to play the leading role. Sex isn't about glossy hair, smooth thighs and inflated boobs. It isn't about a face plastered with makeup or a body trussed up in expensive lingerie. It's about feeling close to someone and relaxing in the knowledge that there's nothing you can't laugh about with them – be it your wobbly tummy or their hairy toes. Think of your body in terms of how it can make you and your partner feel, not how it looks. It's difficult to enjoy the experience if you're preoccupied with the size of your backside. Look at sex for what it is – don't build it into a performance that could win Oscars for direction, sound quality and acting. At the Oscars, there are always losers, but when you and your partner both begin to relax and deal with your body worries, then everyone's a winner.

Finally, and importantly, we need to feel confident within our relationships: if we don't, we accept more and strive for less. A man may accept his cheating wife because he feels that his balding head and beer belly mean he can't do any better. A woman may stay with her abusive husband because her self-confidence has been battered to the point at which she feels nobody else will want her if she left him – safer to stick with a bad relationship than to take the chance of finding a good one.

Leaving, and aspiring for more, contains an element of risk. When our self-esteem is low, we aren't good at taking risks because we don't have the confidence to believe in ourselves. We think we are destined either to stick with a partner who isn't right for us or be alone; the first option sounds marginally better. But, you need to test this theory to prove it wrong. Look at your fears logically. Think of all you have to offer as a person and weigh them against the chances of being alone for the rest of your life. Don't be afraid to be alone for a while, it can be just the tonic you need to build the confidence to come out ready to face the relationship roulette table.

When we feel we aren't worth much, we feel we don't deserve much, so, consequently, we don't aspire for much, and of course we don't achieve much. It's easy to see how the pattern develops. But it's harder to break it. If, for years, you have felt that you simply don't deserve the achievements that others enjoy, it's hard to start believing that you do. But that's what you have to do. Don't feel that your appearance dictates which rung of the career ladder you should be on. Or who you should be dating. Or what car you should be driving. It's easy to blame others for stereotyping us in this way, but, ultimately, it's up to you to turn the stereotype on its head and redefine people's impression of you.

You're worth more than a tired old cliché telling you that fat girls are jolly, funny types who the boys don't fancy, or that girls don't go for skinny men. Think outside the cliché and create your own PR package. Stereotypes and clichés become irrelevant once you begin to discard them and build your self-esteem. Simply choose to believe that you are worth more.

TAKE AWAYS

By now it should be clear that liking yourself means understanding that how you feel about your body is as important as how you look.

We dwell on the aesthetic value of our bodies and forget that they are functional too. So, while we should be enjoying things like swimming, dancing or sex, we are more concerned with how we look while we do it, which can influence the way we feel and behave in relationships, from meeting new people to being intimate in the bedroom. We discussed the terror that runs through us the first time that someone sees us naked and also the need to acknowledge that we're probably not the only one with hang-ups about our naked body. So, to feel better about the way you look in relation to other people:

- See your body as functional *as well as* aesthetic
- Recognise that you are not the only one with body insecurities
- Understand that the way things look don't necessarily affect the way they feel.

Now since a part of this chapter has been devoted to sex some of the take aways that follow are a bit more spicy than usual. So here goes:

TASK 1

Based on what you have learnt from this chapter, consider the assumptions that you think make you feel uncomfortable or anxious in social situations. Remember, the key to dealing with anxieties about social situations is to look at where they stem from. In getting to the core of your negative beliefs and assumptions you'll be on your way to minimising your anxiety. Once you've identified the assumptions that are holding you back, it's just a matter of challenging them, then finding alternative thoughts and beliefs that are more useful and constructive. For example:

Assumptions that make me anxious in social situations	Problem with this type of assumption	Alternative thoughts to counter this assumption
People will take one look at how big my nose is and it'll be like school all over again. No one will like me	*I am jumping to conclusions. There is no evidence that this person won't like me because of my nose. By having this negative expectation I am more likely to act defensively and give the wrong impression about myself. This assumption will make me focus on what I don't like about myself instead of the interesting things I love about myself*	*My nose does not dictate how I interact with people! I do! If I am confident and give people insights into who I am and the things I like about myself, that's what they'll focus on. If they have a problem with the size of my nose, I doubt they're the type of person I'd like to be friends with anyway*

Continue the table, making a note of all the beliefs that cause you anxiety. Ask yourself how realistic they are, and how they make you feel and react.

TASK 2

You may not like this initially, but bear with me. To feel comfortable naked with someone else, you need to feel comfortable naked on your own. Stand in front of a mirror and focus on the five parts of your body you said you liked about yourself in the list you made in chapter 1. Now fill the bath with bubbles, bath salts or whatever relaxes you, and enjoy a nice long soak. While you are relaxing, remember the things you said you liked about yourself, and focus on them. Tell yourself why you like them. Now look at what you don't like, and ask yourself who or what has taught you not to like them. Try to find something positive about those parts of your body, either how they look or how they make you feel. Stay in the bath until you're completely relaxed. Now, get out, get dry and put on a dressing-gown. Stand in front of the mirror again and close your eyes. Take off the dressing-gown and focus again on those parts of you that you really like.

Now open your eyes.

What do you feel?

_____

_____

_____

Are there parts of your body you feel embarrassed about? If yes, why?

_____

_____

_____

Are there parts of your body that you would not like someone to touch?

_____

_____

_____

If yes, why?

_____

_____

_____

What is the worst thing that could happen if someone saw you naked?
Think hard about this and take your answer to its logical conclusion:

_____

_____

_____

Are your fears realistic? Do you think that you could cope with that
happening?

_____

_____

_____

If yes, how?

_____

_____

_____

If no, why not?

_____

_____

_____

Now you have begun to rewrite the script with regard to how you
look and how you value yourself. You will underline the idea that your
body can feel wonderful, even though it may not be perfect. While

you're doing this exercise, if you catch yourself feeling negative about some aspect of your appearance ask yourself where the negativity comes from and acknowledge all the things it is denying you. I am not expecting an overnight miracle where you love everything you see when you look in the mirror – but I know that if you take the time to look at yourself realistically, challenging your negative beliefs, you will value yourself as a person, and learn to like your body.

Now go out and buy some underwear that you would never normally buy. Enjoy the experience – choose something that draws attention to those parts of your body that you like. When you get home, put it on and stand in front of the mirror. Tell yourself what you like about the way you look. Better yet, stand in front of your partner and ask if they like what they see.

TASK 3

Don't forget: next time you are intimate, focus on what feels good to the *touch* both for your partner and yourself.

Chapter Six

YOUR BODY 9–5: BODY IMAGE AND THE WORKPLACE

I was standing in the ladies' loo trying to pluck out a giant black hair that had sprouted between my eyebrows when Felicity Lush, James's line manager, came in. She was what most people would call beautiful, about 5'7", long shiny brown hair, big green eyes and a perfect body. She always dressed immaculately and looked as if she had just walked off the set of a hair-conditioner commercial. Even though Felicity and I had started on the same day, she progressed up the corporate ladder a lot quicker than me. No surprise, really, since all the good jobs in the company seemed to go to people like Felicity, attractive, successful, the type of person you dreamt of being when you grew up. Felicity had it all: above-average brains, above-average looks and a wonderful above-average career to go with it. Everyone liked her, and no matter how much I hated to admit it, she was always really nice and lovely to talk to. She smiled at me and began trying to wash some blue ink off her perfectly manicured little finger. 'So, how have you been, Sarah?'

'Oh, you know, same shit different day.' I had no idea why I was talking in bumper stickers but felt that I needed to be cool.

'So you're getting bored with your job?'

'Well, it's not that challenging, really, sitting in a purple cubicle all day crunching numbers for overpriced marketing accounts.'

'You'd rather do something more creative?'

'I guess, I don't know. The people in the creative department seem a lot more, um . . . creative than me,' and thinner and prettier than me – I thought to myself.

'Don't be silly. James and the other guys in our team are always going on about how witty you are. Listen, there are some openings coming up in my department. Why don't you send your CV through? I'll take a look at it and we can see about a move for you in a direction that's more challeng—'

'Um, sorry, what did you say James said about me?'

'That you seem really nice and funny.'

'What . . . funny in a three stooges sort of way or funny in an "I feel happy when I'm around her" sort of way?'

'Er . . . the second one?'

'Really?'

'Do you like James?'

'Who, me? No! Are you insane! Maybe a little . . . Yes, actually, I do . . . a lot.'

I made Felicity swear on her French manicure that she wouldn't tell James how I felt about him, and Felicity insisted I should tell him because we'd make a cute couple and that I should also apply for the job because I clearly wasn't happy in my purple cubicle. Our conversation was interrupted by the sound of flushing and we both walked out.

After our loo encounter, every time I caught Felicity's eye she would do this weird winky thing and every time I caught sight of James I would hide for fear that he'd found out about me . . .

In recent years the workplace has changed from being the place where we go to earn a living to a place where we go to challenge ourselves, live out our goals and develop aspirations about who we'd like to be. Romances are played out by water-coolers, friends are made over photocopiers and enemies gossiped about at the local Starbucks during coffee breaks. The way we present ourselves in the workplace has become an important issue, both socially and in relation to the career ladder. If we feel that we aren't able to present ourselves in the best light due to a poor body image then this can affect not only how we interact with others at work but also our career aspirations. We buy into the myth that beautiful people are more competent and successful than their non-beautiful counterparts.

Some people just look as if they're destined to do well – don't they? A winning smile, glossy hair, perfect body, it's hard to see how they could go wrong. Or put it this way – imagine a really successful person, for example the managing director of a massive company. Or somebody who has achieved all their ambitions. The image you see probably isn't of someone with below-average looks, whether they're male or female. We assume success goes hand in hand with the way we look. And we tell ourselves, 'If only I was thinner, fatter, shorter, taller, I'd get that promotion,' or 'There's no point in bringing up my ideas at meetings – I'll only be outshone by Rachel, who's always confident in meetings and, of course, beautiful.' We excuse our own failure, by blaming the way we look, and we undermine the competence of the gorgeous girl in Accounts by attributing her success to the way she looks.

So, do looks really matter in the workplace? Well, the truth is that they can make a difference in the success or failure of someone's career. Research has shown that people who are seen as attractive are occasionally favoured in the workplace. They are offered assistance more readily, find better jobs and can gain more influence on others than less attractive people. Good-looking people are seen as more sociable – and they are generally more confident, which means that they are likely to have good social skills and take more risks to advance their careers. So in fact what we are talking about again boils down not to better bodies but to better body image. Attractive people are seen in a positive light, which gives them confidence in themselves, which in turn improves their social skills which means that they're seen in a positive light. What makes people attractive is their confidence and spark, and it's this which we can find in ourselves if we improve our self-perception. The reality is that attractive people fare well in life not only because of how others see them but, much more importantly, because of how they see themselves. Something that all of us can change no matter what we look like.

Success and Beauty

Many researchers have looked into the way that we, as a culture, associate beauty with qualities such as goodness and success, and ugliness with things like badness and failure, and, surprise surprise, it all starts in childhood. As we've seen, many of the core beliefs we form about the world around us are derived from messages that we receive as children. If we read in every fairytale that the heroes were beautiful and the villains ugly, in every cartoon we watched the winner was pretty and the loser was unattractive we make the connection that pretty = good and not pretty = bad.

You might think that as we grow up, we would reach a point where we could accept that, rationally, just as princesses don't sleep for a hundred years and frogs don't turn into princes when someone kisses them, it is unlikely that all beautiful people are good and successful. But the truth is that this story continues to be force-fed to us long after we've grown out of fairytales. The movie industry and other media play a profound role in dictating what our lives should look like: physical flaws are rarely presented except in relation to personality flaws. Even if at the start of the movie the hero is an unattractive geek, he is always transformed into a good-looking hunk before the final credits. Handicapped people or people with disfigurements are practically never given central roles, and on the rare occasions that they are, the focus is on their handicap rather than on them as an individual. And, of course, the notion that success has a pretty face is fed into other aspects of our lives: from company brochures displaying smug bank managers with perfect teeth, to children's TV presenters who might have parallel careers as glamour models, we are told that we 'should' look a certain way to be successful. We are sold the idea that there are 'professional' ways to dress and 'professional' hairstyles that will help us achieve this. Any way you look at it, we are constantly bombarded with images that show successful people looking only one way: attractive.

Research has shown that when we feel less confident about our appearance, we believe we should aspire to less and deserve less. There is evidence, for example, that adolescents with acne have lower career aspirations than their peers. This sense of inadequacy comes from core beliefs and assumptions that life is better for attractive people, that successful people have particular physical assets and if you don't have them it's unlikely that you'll succeed. If you maintain such core beliefs it is hard to develop the psychological traits such as good self-esteem, confidence and social skills that you need to be successful. If you believe that people are repelled by the size of your ears, you won't have the self-assurance you need to go out and grab opportunities or take chances, which are key factors in career progression. It's as if our thoughts programme us to aspire to less. Years ago, people were made to believe that certain careers were out of reach because of their social or economic background. Today our aspirations may be dictated by our physical appearance. If we see ourselves as not good enough, we will feel unable to obtain what we see as the right of the 'beautiful', such as a high-status job.

If we feel bad about the way we look, then odds are that we will also feel negatively about how much we can achieve in life. We may expect disappointment and thus fear even the thought of something new because we simply don't have faith in ourselves. Recent research sponsored by NAAFA (National Association to Advance Fat Acceptance), a San Francisco-based advocacy organisation, showed that only 9 per cent of top male executives are overweight. This might be attributable to discrimination in hiring, but it could just as easily point towards a lack of career confidence in overweight males. Our society has a deep-rooted belief that good things come to the beautiful, and it's hard to get out of that mentality. But hard doesn't mean impossible. It is possible, and it's up to us to separate our career aspirations from the way we look. When you consider the two, there shouldn't be a link. Does a man's great skin make him a better lawyer? Will a woman's pert breasts make her a better doctor? Of course not.

More often than not, we ourselves make the link between our appearance and how much we can achieve, and it's up to us to break it. Yes, research shows that people tend to respond favourably to the more attractive, but it also shows that they will see you as more attractive if you are confident and self-assured. If you feel that the mole on your nose is the most important, most obvious thing about you, that is what it will become. When you choose to define yourself by a single feature you dislike, this minimises the essence of who you are. When we focus on a perceived deficit we believe that others will do the same and will be unable to take us seriously. This type of thinking ultimately leads to low self-esteem and insecurity. If, however, you see the mole as a small part of who you are that couldn't even begin to define you as a person, then the sum of your assets is what you and everyone else focuses on and consequently that mole is of no importance to you or anyone else. Don't let your body worry dictate how you are received by other people. You are the one who should be dictating your impact on others. So next time you walk into a boardroom, don't let your body insecurities become an issue. You're not there to debate how big your bum looks, so why should it be relevant to your success in business?

The Beauty Contest

After my fabulous loo encounter I rang Trudy and Antonio to tell them that James thought I was funny and convened an emergency lunch conference to analyse in detail what this meant. We met at Luigi's sandwich shop where Luigi greeted me with a giant mocha latte – 'Your usual!' he said warmly (he was clearly relieved that I had given up my diet). The other two had already arrived and were sitting at a round table next to a CD player pumping out cheerful Christmas carols. I sat down, took off my scarf and reeled off a detailed description of what had happened. 'You should so apply for that job!' said Trudy.

'You should so apply some lip-gloss and get over there and kiss that James!' said Antonio.

We giggled and as I sipped my latte I ran through a list of reasons why these ideas were not viable. 'There are a dozen people in the office who are a lot better qualified and frankly a lot cuter than me. I mean, who am I kidding? The competition's fierce. Marjory Simpson has just got a great pair of fake boobs and Amy Rydale has lost so much weight you can see her hip-bones when she wears hipsters. Besides, my self-esteem is still a little low because of my weight. Better hold off till I feel better about myself. Then I can think about the job and James . . .'

'OK, now I'm bored,' said Trudy, rolling her eyes.

'What?'

'Listen, Sarah, you're my best friend and I love you, but you really need to get over the fact that the world revolves around the size of your bum. It doesn't, no one cares as much as you, and if you weren't so busy fantasising about how repulsive your body is you might actually open up your eyes and see how many people like you!'

'Yeah, Luigi for one is pining for you over by the sun-dried tomatoes,' added Antonio.

'Listen, Sarah, we discussed this in my psychology class last week. Your problem isn't your life, it's the way you see your life! You don't have to lose weight to prove anything! James and this job are not too good for you!'

'Yeah, they'd be lucky to have her, right, Miss Freud?' giggled Antonio, looking over at Trudy.

I expected myself to say something about how she had no idea what she was talking about and how she wasn't turning me into one of her night class guinea pigs, but instead I just sat there staring blankly at them. I glanced over at Luigi, who was gazing at me while

*he scraped burnt cheese off his toaster, and considered that Trudy
(with all her annoying 'we are the world' type psychobabble) might
have a point.*

'Pass the biscotti,' I snapped.

'Don't be angry, Sarah, we're just trying to help.'

It's not you I'm angry with, I thought to myself . . . it's me.

We all know what happened to Snow White. Her stepmother found out from that blasted mirror that she was
no longer the fairest and, in a fit of jealous rage, ordered
Snow White's death. We all know what it's like to experience jealousy or even resentment of another woman.
Especially when she appears to threaten our career.

Women are conditioned to accept that they are valued
on the basis of appearance far more than men. In a working
environment, most males know that they will be judged on
their intelligence and competence. Most women, however,
feel that the criteria for their assessment are far more
comprehensive than this. They believe that their figure, face
and sex appeal could be called into question. This is because
they are often exposed to a type of self-consciousness to
which most men are oblivious. As discussed in earlier chapters, women's bodies are used to sell almost anything, and
as a consequence we are more likely than men to be aware
of the value judgements made on us. We tend to seek
approval and reassurance from others, while men, valued
for their competence, don't have the same need for such
approval.

In a lot of ways, the whole notion of beauty sustains
competitiveness between women. We have been conditioned so that our identities have at their core how 'pretty'
we are, so we are vulnerable to outside approval, seeking

it from everyone from our partners to our employers. This vulnerability deflates our self-esteem, making our need to compete with other women a 'normal' necessary part of our survival strategy.

This approval-seeking, this race to the top, is carried over into the workplace. And this is where the struggle between women really begins – lipsticks ready at fifty paces, ladies. Because women do feel that they are in constant competition with other women. And the first thing women compete on is looks because we have been taught to value ourselves by them. When we find out that a new female employee is starting in our department the first thing we want to find out about her, whether we admit it or not, is 'What does she look like? Is she a threat to me?' The sad thing is, the biggest insult you can pay yourself is to compete with colleagues on the basis of looks because you are telling yourself that you have nothing else to offer. Even though it seems logical for female colleagues to compete on the basis of their experience, or intelligence, most of the time it comes down to the glossiest hair, girliest giggle, or longest legs.

Again, the reason for this lies in our relationship with the opposite sex. Since in most societies (including our own) men generally control the economic power, women are made to feel that they need to compete with other women for male attention and, consequently, male-dominated resources. Social conditioning tells women that their main goal in life is to find a man, so they see every other woman as competition. Which is why, for many women, going to work entails so much more than just getting up and getting in the car. It means paying immense attention to their appearance and presentation.

The age-old stereotype of females as sex objects rather than as serious contenders in the workplace reinforces the false need for attractiveness. Some male bosses make it hard for women to feel as though they are valued for any other contribution they may be able to make. This is especially true of women who work *for* men and are desired by them. Female subordinates are often seen by men as one of the perks of their position. Even today where cases of harassment in the workplace are dealt with more seriously, this master-servant relationship, where a female secretary panders to her male boss, still exists.

Until relatively recently women in the workplace had only two choices of the type of female employee they could be: (a) the stereotypical blonde but stupid secretary or (b) the dowdy, man-hating battle-axe managing director. Great choice. After realising that femininity and competence were not, as many a stereotype would have us believe, mutually exclusive, we refused to buy that scenario and so we rewrote the job description to suit our needs. Out went the power suits with huge shoulder-pads that acted as male drag, allowing us to 'fit in' with our masculine colleagues and in came women who looked and thought like women – competent employees who believed that their worth lay in their ability. Some of us even cottoned on to the fact that the competition with other women to be the best-looking is demeaning, demoralising and false – because there's no winner. Except, perhaps, for the male employer. He will use this rivalry to keep a woman colleague down by making sure that she takes her eye off the ball for so long that she fails to progress to the point at which she becomes a threat to him.

No matter how we explain the origins of this competition between women we should take some responsibility for the role we play in maintaining it. We can complain about male sexism in the workplace, but many of us reinforce dominant-male ideology every time we step into the office, by placing our value in our looks more than in our skills, by joining in the race against other women. So, how do we avoid competing in this universal beauty contest? For starters, we can challenge some of the so-called truths that society feeds us.

Beauty is not a requirement for success or power. No matter what people would have you believe, you have other, much more important assets that will help you attain your goals. Take a look at some of the most successful female politicians of our time – they have so much to say (whether you agree with it or not) that their appearance rarely comes into play.

Beauty is not the most important asset that a woman has to offer. The facts speak for themselves: girls consistently achieve higher grades than boys at both primary and secondary school. Women are now major players in the highest levels of industry and commerce, with female entrepreneurs starting up a significant proportion of successful new business ventures. Women are hard-working and have ingenuity. In agricultural societies, even when given unequal resources, women's harvests at least equal those of their male counterparts!

Beauty is not an ideal to be aspired to – like freedom, justice or equality. Rather, it is a fleeting, changing whim based on so many diverse opinions and values that it ultimately becomes an arbitrary concept. It is also therefore a weak foundation for self-esteem. Simply stated, aspiring to be beautiful is futile if you wish to feel better about yourself.

Controlling how you look doesn't mean controlling your life. Managing or changing the way you look only works if it improves your body image. The traits required to succeed in any career have a lot more to do with capabilities than your appearance.

The artificial link between beauty and success is a result of a negative assumption about the way the two are related, fuelled by low self-esteem and poor body image. By challenging the negative thoughts that give so much credence to the way we look and so little importance to who we are, we move closer to both a better body image and higher self-esteem. Look at the criteria you set yourself. How logical is it to dream that if you were prettier, you would be taken more seriously at meetings or handed a promotion? Totally illogical. The importance of our own looks is up to us. If we give people nothing else to comment on, then that is all we will be judged on. If others are impressed by our skills and warm to our personality, the importance of our appearance lessens. By blaming failures in the workplace on our appearance, we are missing the point and denying ourselves the opportunity to learn and grow from our mistakes. By equating success in the workplace with beauty, again we reduce genuine achievement to something as trivial as physical appearance. Perhaps we always think of successful people as attractive because some who are obviously rich and successful, like models and Hollywood film stars, are attractive. But it's important to remember that these people, by the very nature of the fact that their jobs involve being in the public eye, probably got there partly because of their looks in the first place. Celebrity fame is only one kind of success; a quick look at the world's richest people or those who have reached amazing goals will reveal that most of their achievements had nothing to do with appearance.

Ultimately, it is up to you how you are treated and respected at work – not your boss, your colleagues, and certainly not the size of your bottom. You dictate what you will accept from the people you work with. If you challenge the core beliefs that led you to believe that your value lies in how big your boobs are rather than your work experience, you will be way ahead of the game because you are refusing to play it.

Here are some things to try next time you catch yourself holding back in your career because of your appearance:

- Make a list of the reasons why you think you are qualified for the job or promotion and next to that a list of the reasons why you think you're not. If the former is longer, put in your application. What are you waiting for? If the latter is longer, look into improving your skills and challenge negative thoughts about appearance, if they appear on your list.
- Make a list of the people you admire in your field. Beside their names write down what you think makes them good at what they do. I'll bet the words 'straight teeth' don't appear anywhere.
- Ask yourself where you would like to be career-wise in five years' time. Now ask yourself how you plan to get there without putting yourself up for promotions and/or new jobs.
- Finally ask yourself what the worst-case scenario would be if you were to apply for a job and not get it. Compare that with stagnating for fear of rejection. What's the worst-case scenario now?

Checklists

Most of us have in mind a checklist as we go through life.

First, we want a great job, with a large office overlooking the Thames in London or Central Park in New York. Or we want to be a great dolphin trainer or the first person to walk on Mars. By ticking off number one on the list we often tick off other aspirations, such as the dream car, the sprawling country manor and the cottage in the country.

Second, we want to find the perfect relationship. We want a man who irons, cooks and cleans, while he isn't off saving young children in poor countries or modelling in Milan. He has to be able to quote Shakespeare, in a Barry White voice, of course. He has to love our mother, be friends with our father. And he has to be a genius in the bedroom. Or we want to find a woman with Heidi Klum's body and Carol Vorderman's brain. She has to love football, *and* support our team. She has to be able to tell a few dirty jokes, but not too many. She has to accept everything we say, without misinterpreting, analysing or dissecting it. In short, we want to find that special person who is just made for us, and we want them to want us too. There are other things on the checklist too. We want a great supportive group of friends, who are always there for us. We want the best wardrobe in town. We want to raise three perfectly behaved, beautiful children. We want to be the first woman to climb Mount Everest in stilettos. We want to be the first beer-bellied lager lout to turn professional footballer at the age of thirty-five. Basically, we all have a roadmap of where we want our life to go, the ambitions we want to fulfil.

Sometimes, though, life doesn't work out exactly the way we planned it. Sometimes the dream husband turns out to be lovely and kind but a bit of a slob who works down the local sewage plant, rather than modelling in Milan. Sometimes the two-seater sex-mobile sports car turns out to be a clapped-out Fiesta. And sometimes, just sometimes, we find ourselves filing in a hot stuffy office rather than communicating with dolphins. When we feel we aren't fulfilling our dreams, or crossing off any of our checklist items, it can affect the way we feel about ourselves, lowering our self-esteem and confidence. Even more importantly, when we don't feel great about ourselves we can feel as though we don't really deserve to accomplish any of our goals.

We start to wonder why we haven't reached all our dreams, and when we're looking for something to blame, the first thing we turn to is our appearance. A recent study revealed that the majority of women who were dissatisfied with their body image tended to blame their looks for other disappointments in their lives including career setbacks. And the men are just as bad, a survey by *Men's Health* magazine concluded that 75 per cent of men are unhappy with their body shape and its impact on their life success. It becomes an easy scapegoat when we're not feeling so great about where we are in life. As a consequence, our body image can also dictate how much we dare to dream, and the risks we will take to get there. Put simply, we set our sights lower if we feel unhappy with the way we look. Our body image has a huge effect on where we think we should be in life because our appearance is the most obvious thing about us.

The real problem with this reasoning, however, begins when we start *wishing* we were more beautiful. Whether it is during adolescence or following a knockback in our career, once we fantasise about a nicer body, smoother skin or finer features, in the hopes that these things will make us happier, we deny ourselves the self-acceptance that can make us happier. Worse yet, wishing for a 'new you' means that you are forced to degrade the 'you' that you are now, the more you wish to look like someone different, the more unhappy you become with the person you are right now. So, what ultimately makes you unhappy is not your physical appearance but your wish to be a different you.

We give our appearance far too much importance in the grand scheme of things. When we ask ourselves why we didn't speak up at that meeting, we blame our fat thighs. When we wonder why *her* research proposals were used instead of ours, we blame our height. It's far easier to criticise and assess the outside than the inside. And this approach lets us off the hook. We don't bother to look for the true causes of our problems. Perhaps we didn't get that promotion because the boss objects to us spending half the day gossiping by the water fountain. Perhaps someone better qualified than us responded to the advertisement. We need to look deeper, rather than blame the outer layers, or we won't give ourselves the opportunity to address the real reasons for our disappointments. When we blame our appearance for a disappointment in the workplace we are scapegoating – we need to blame something for the fact that our career isn't going as we'd like and as we feel let down by our looks anyway, we blame them. It's natural to look for reasons to explain away a disappointment or rejection, but jumping to the conclusion that your appearance is to blame when you don't have any evidence of this, is not the answer. In fact, it only further underlines the negative, irrational thoughts about our body image, which made us feel bad in the first place!

Risk-taking

Nobody ever ticked off everything on that life checklist without taking a few risks. Study after study will tell you that the most successful people are the most confident risk-takers. They are prepared to gamble a little, and don't always play it safe. But diving head first into something, when you're not sure of the consequences, requires confidence in your ability to survive, in case the outcome isn't as you'd hoped. We all know someone who grabs any opportunity and goes for it. They might be a friend who can pitch an idea at a meeting without any sign of nervousness, or a colleague who is continually making rash decisions, against the boss's wishes, but who always ends up sealing the deal.

To take risks, we need to believe in ourselves. And when we feel down about the way we look, or preoccupied with one aspect of our appearance, we do not have that confidence. As we define ourselves in terms of the way we look, we feel incompetent, inadequate, and take the safe option. We might dive into the pool, but we make sure we're close to the side. We know it means we won't become fast, strong, brave swimmers, but at least we won't drown. Playing it safe seems like the best policy when we feel insecure. But, ironically, the only way to get rid of the insecurities is to face the fears that are holding you back and start taking a few risks.

First, you need to acknowledge that you are so much more than the way you look. The real you is about what you do, what you love, what you hate, what scares you, what makes you laugh, what makes you sad. It's about the exams you have passed, the people whose lives you have touched, the experience you have gained, the lessons you have learnt. It's about those Girl Guide badges you were so proud of, or the holiday photos that still make you cry with laughter. Really, the excess flab on your arms is irrelevant. Define yourself by the things that matter. Know what your real weaknesses are. Perhaps you could be more efficient. Perhaps you interrupt people too much. Perhaps you need to contribute more during meetings. Accepting what you love about yourself, and your faults, is a step towards lessening the importance of that body anxiety, and you can start to see yourself in terms of who you are, not what you look like.

Second, to build up the confidence to take risks, imagine the worst-case scenario. When something scares us, we gasp, 'Oh, God, there's no way I'm doing that!' then banish the idea immediately. Instead, follow the scenario to its logical conclusion. You might see a job advertised in your department that offers more money, more holiday leave and a bigger office. You want to apply for it, but you can't comprehend how awful you'd feel if you didn't get it. You imagine people in the department snickering and thinking, How dare she think she was good enough for a job like that? So you ignore the pang of excitement every time you walk past the notice on the bulletin board. No harm done, you assure yourself, your life is still intact. But you've let yourself down because you assumed the worst and didn't take the time to discover what your worst-case scenario would mean.

Instead of shrinking in terror at the thought of applying for the job, follow the story to its various endings. You might apply and get the job, and be so successful you end up running the company. Or you might apply and not get the job. What's the worst that can happen? Will your heart stop beating? Will your lungs collapse? Will the world self-combust? Will you become a social outcast? No, no, no and no. The worst that can happen is that you will walk away without a new job but with fresh experience of interviews that you can learn from and use the next time you apply for a job. Will others laugh at you for trying? No – but frankly if they did it would be because of their own insecurities. In applying you've lost nothing, and probably gained a little confidence, because taking risks is something to be proud of, even when things don't go your way. And next time it won't be so hard because you know what the worst-case scenario is.

When it comes to careers, if you don't ever take a risk you may miss out on a job that really fulfils you, or that will help you develop and grow as a person. Next time you find yourself holding back, ask yourself, 'What do I have to lose?' Odds are, the only way you'll lose is by limiting yourself, by not taking a chance.

Rewriting Your Script

*E*ver since I spoke to Felicity, and subsequent lunch summit with Trudy and Antonio, I haven't been able to stop thinking about changing jobs. But I keep catching myself thinking back to a meeting with a careers adviser when I was fifteen . . .

I had been sent to see Mr Roberts because I was caught passing notes about the music teacher's botched nose job during band practice. 'That's it Sawah go to Mistaw Woberts offwice now!' she snorted. Mr Roberts had a fairly broad job description: he was careers adviser, student counsellor, filled in for the art teacher when she was ill, and coached the girls' hockey team. His ability to perform in any of these settings was spread pretty thinly, to say the least.

I walked into his tiny dark office and sat down on a hard wooden stool covered with a stained orange cushion with 'Seize the day . . .' embroidered on it. He sat across from me and gave me an ominous glare. 'So, Sarah, being disruptive during band practice, were we?'

I nodded, refraining from pointing out how 'we' had done nothing, rather 'I' had been disruptive while 'he' was probably off losing another hockey game.

'You see, Sarah, pupils like you, average, unremarkable pupils, often become disruptive as a means of gaining attention. Now, I know you aren't particularly athletic, attractive or, indeed, popular, but you shouldn't let this make you feel envious of others. We all have our strengths and weaknesses, and we use them best when we know our place. You, for example, are unlikely to excel in a career that requires leadership, creativity or above-average intelligence. Rather, you should aim for things you can reach . . . so as to avoid disappointment. You can be the person behind the scenes, the one who supports those with the ability to reach important positions, the less charming, less qualified but just as important team-player . . . Understand?'

When he had finished his little speech, I remember just sitting there in shock. I felt deflated, defeated and sad. I nodded and asked if I could go. He smiled and said that he was happy we had this important talk.

As I reached the door I remember him calling back, 'Oh, and you might want to consider trying out for the hockey team. It will help you lose some weight and improve your body shape.' Ever since that day I have sort of seen myself as frumpy, as average, as unremarkable, and as not deserving more . . . It occurred to me now that I had been the one who was sabotaging myself all along. Trudy and Antonio may have been right. Maybe I could have a better job, maybe Mr Roberts was wrong, maybe . . . Maybe I would apply for the job in Felicity's department after all . . .

We all go through life with ideas about who we are and how we should behave. These 'scripts' often derive from the messages we have received from others throughout our lives about how we *should* act and who we *should* be. Your script may say that you're the black sheep of the family, or that you're the bespectacled nerd who was great at science, or the chubby kid whom everyone wants as their friend but no one wants as their girlfriend. If your script is limiting you, or hindering your ability to see yourself as you really are, you need to rewrite it before you can succeed in a work situation. Now, as with most major life changes, that is easier said than done. If you've spent your life seeing yourself as someone who wasn't good enough or pretty enough to succeed, you may find it difficult to see yourself as anything else. Moreover, you may have become comfortable with the script because it makes life predictable.

So if you've always been the frumpy but clever girl at school who never had many friends but was great at algebra, you may find that this script dominates you at work. You stay late every night but never go to the pub for drinks because you expect others not to like you. Or if your script said that your older brother was the leader in the family and you were the follower, you may shy away from showing initiative on work projects because your script has convinced you that you couldn't cope with a leading role.

The funny thing is that often, in such scenarios, the opposite happens. When we make a major lifestyle change that involves meeting new people rewriting our script becomes easier. All of a sudden we are surrounded by people waiting for *us* to tell them who we are, rather than people who think they know us and thus have expectations about us. So, a girl who's always been teased about being blonde and ditsy by people in her town might start a new job far from home. And in her suitcase, along with her toothbrush and the pink pyjamas her mum has just bought, she'll pack a massive great insecurity core belief about how others see her. She might not be blonde or ditsy any more, but childhood labels stick, even when they cease to be true. When she meets her new workmates, she'll probably make the same assumptions about their assumptions that she normally makes when she meets new people: 'She thinks I'm stupid', 'He thinks I'm easy and a pushover.' But slowly, as she begins to rewrite the script by challenging these views of herself, and showing her new friends aspects of her personality that she feels are important, she'll realise that none of them sees her in terms of her old script. She'll realise that she is valued for who she is, not criticised for how she appears, which will probably give her the confidence to excel, leaving behind the script that was limiting her success.

This type of self-discovery is particularly relevant when we start our first job. Not only do we tend to make a new group of friends, who see us in a different way from our family or childhood friends, we get a new sense of worth from being valued for our ability. We have the potential to become more confident about the way we look and discover how much we have to offer emotionally and intellectually as well as physically. In fact, the way that new people respond to us and feel about us is usually a good indicator of who we are because their judgements come free of bias or prior knowledge.

The good news is that our scripts are not cast in iron. If we are willing to change our perspective on what we experience, a positive editing of them will follow. To start the editing, try the following:

1. Learn to see yourself in terms of your current achievements and personal assets, rather than through past experiences and comments that have made you feel bad about yourself.
2. Learn to identify and challenge the unhelpful shoulds and have-tos that are limiting you and the aspirations you have for yourself.
3. Know that people can change. Just because you didn't excel at school doesn't mean you won't be great at the career you choose.
4. Take control of your present and put the past in perspective. You might have let your looks stop you auditioning for the heroine in the school play but that isn't a valid reason to let them stop you applying for a job you want.
5. Learn how to take pride in your achievements and skills – and know that these are not related to your appearance.

Another great way to rewrite your script is by making a body-image insecurity into your trademark. If you really can't forget your crooked teeth, or that mole on your cheek, turn it into something that allows you to stand out from the crowd in a positive way. Looking different doesn't necessarily mean looking bad. Reinterpret the 'flawed' feature as an interesting, important, unique part of you. But remember, your perception of your appearance, not your appearance itself, is responsible for the negative feelings you hold about yourself, if you want to see a difference when you look into the mirror that is what you need to work on.

Consider this: Cindy Crawford was told by every agency she visited as a young aspiring model to remove the mole on her face. Eventually she became one of the world's top supermodels, famous for, you've guessed it, that mole. In 1946, Sylvester Stallone was born. Unfortunately, a forceps accident left him with a paralysed lip, chin and tongue.

Years later, a star is born featuring in blockbusters like *Rocky* and *Rambo*. He became an instant sex symbol and women went weak at the knees over, surprise, surprise, his droopy lip, and slow, drawling voice. If an actor in image-obsessed Hollywood can turn facial paralysis into a sex-symbol trademark, there's nothing you can't put a positive spin on.

When people talk about you, don't be 'that woman with the fat bum who's always shuffling along, looking at the floor', become 'that hot woman from the office with a bum like J-Lo's'. And speaking of Jennifer Lopez, she is another fine example of someone who has turned a body feature that some might criticise into an asset, single-handedly universalising the Latino love of the bigger bottom. Before Miss Lopez flounced into our lives, women were agonising over ways to downsize their bottoms. Now, they're queuing up to have fat pumped into them. If they can do it, so can you. Embrace the wonky nose, or dreaded mole, or crooked teeth. Let it become your trademark, the thing that people remember you for – in a good way.

There are challenges in life that we all go through. Some are compulsory (think illness, exams and embarrassing family members), some aren't. But we put ourselves through the optional challenges because we know that, in the long run, they're good for us – getting a new job, or taking on a new, demanding project. We know that to get ahead we must make these changes. And they're tough enough on their own. But to make things even harder, we throw ourselves into the world of work, or 'the real world', as our fathers call it (as in 'You need to start living in the . . .'), with a whole travel bag full of insecurities about who we are and just how much we are capable of achieving. And the way we look is one of the first things we begin to find fault with, especially when everything seems to land at the feet of the better-looking people of the world. This kicks off a vicious circle of feelings of inadequacy and lack of confidence which can result in failure which worsens our feelings of inadequacy. Most of us feel that in a strange way, the way we look correlates directly to how much money we can earn, or how much influence we can wield.

As we've seen, the way to change this negative thinking is to make the decision to withdraw from the competition that says the winner is the most beautiful. You need to pull out of that tournament, so rip up your entry form and demand a refund on the entry money you paid, because if we do compete in the workplace, we need to compete with our colleagues on terms of ability, regardless of their sex. Long term, the only way to gain respect and self-confidence is to use your personality to win you those gold medals. Whenever we face a new challenge in life, we need to be able to remind ourselves that the most important thing about us is what we can do, not what we look like.

Although life challenges can seem like a potential lethal injection for our body confidence, they can actually be the best cure for a little bit of body-image battering. Taking on and coping with a new work situation allows us to re-write the script, to pack up those old labels, and leave them somewhere they won't be found. It gives us a chance to grow out of 'big-ears' or 'half-pint'. Meeting new people can also help you challenge a negative script – people can only really judge you from the minute you introduce yourself, and unless you want to tell them that you strongly believe that the size of your butt will dictate your earning power for the next ten years then they're never going to know. So give it your best shot, and be the you that you want to be.

TAKE AWAYS

This chapter dealt with how your body image can dictate your aspirations and limit your potential to achieve. Successful people come in all shapes and sizes and the keys to success are in our self-belief and skills. Ban self-defeating thoughts and focus on building that all-important belief in yourself.

TASK 1

The point of this exercise is to show how appearance is irrelevant in evaluating someone's achievements. It's designed to help you challenge negative core beliefs about how your looks relate to your personal strengths and qualities. Make a list of some successful people you admire, write down their achievements, then rate them in terms of their appearance.

Example:

Successful person I admire	Why I admire them	Looks out of 10
Mother Teresa	Selfless missionary work	
Nelson Mandela	Idealist, freedom-fighter, inspiration	

How does it feel to judge people you admire by their appearance? I bet you feel silly even thinking about how attractive they are, that what they look like is irrelevant because of who they are and what they've achieved. Now put your name on the list of people you admire and list the things that make you inspirational. Remember this next time you minimise your achievements in relation to how you look.

TASK 2

Now in Table 2.2 write a list of career aspirations and next to each write how important your looks are in attaining that goal, both directly and indirectly. In cases where you feel that they do count take the idea to its logical conclusion, then see how far you believe they are hindering you in achieving your goals. Table 2.1 provides an example:

TABLE 2.1

Career goals	Importance of your appearance in attaining these goals	Is this belief realistic?	Is it hindering you in achieving your goals?
Playing professional basketball	*Very important; need to be tall*	*Yes, the vast majority of players are very tall*	*Not really. I'm coaching my son's team so I'm still able to enjoy the game even though I'm a few inches too short to play professionally*

| Becoming manager of my department at work | Important: all managers are attractive and likeable | Well, maybe not – our CEO is not exactly Angelina Jolie and at least a couple of managers aren't very attractive | Yes. By minimising what I have to offer in relation to how I look, I'm undermining all the other qualities that would make me a good manager and stopping myself achieving my goals |

TABLE 2.2

Career goals	Importance of your appearance in attaining these goals	Is this belief realistic?	Is it hindering you in achieving your goals?

TASK 3

This exercise is based on Task 3 in chapter 4. In the same way that you used guided imagery to help you imagine yourself exposing a part of your body that you were anxious about, here you will use it to help you feel more confident in the workplace. First unplug the phone, turn off the TV, lie down and relax. Prepare by doing the relaxation exercise from page 130. Close your eyes and imagine yourself applying for a new job either within your department or outside. Focus on what you see around you and how you feel, all the time reminding yourself of how safe and comfortable and positive you feel. Now bring into the imagery your worst fear – not getting the job or someone more attractive than you getting the job. Pay attention to what you are thinking and remember to challenge any negative thoughts related to your body image. See yourself handling the situation comfortably, feeling positive about having applied for the job, no matter the outcome. Now see yourself walking around happily – catch a glimpse of yourself in a full-length mirror as you walk past it and see yourself smiling and feeling positive. Tell yourself that you like who you are and that what matters in your career is *who* you are, which is much more important than how you look. When you are ready, open your eyes.

You will probably need to do this twice a week until you feel confident about your career or your career aspirations.

Chapter Seven

PLASTIC SURGERY AND MAKEUP: CHANGING THE PERSON LOOKING BACK

I put the phone down, screamed, 'Damn, I'm good!' and got up on the sofa and started dancing. I couldn't believe it, I had just been told that I made the shortlist for interview for the vacancy in Felicity's department! They were actually, seriously considering me for the job! 'I am woman hear me roar!' I shouted, as I did the Macarena on the couch. I began to fantasise about working next to James, seeing him every day, hearing him every day – smelling him every day . . . snogging him every . . . when all of a sudden my wonderful fantasy was interrupted by the entryphone buzzing. It was my mother announcing that she was downstairs and would I please hurry up and open the door because she was freezing. I'd forgotten I'd promised to go Christmas shopping with her this weekend. I put on my pink bathrobe, patted down my hair and tried to take off last night's mascara with my finger and some spit as I ran to open the door.

I opened to find her standing there, impeccably dressed and made-up as usual, she walked in, kissed me, pointed out that my roots needed doing and then sat on the sofa. There was something different about her, but I couldn't quite put my finger on what it was.

'Guess what, Mum, I've been shortlisted for that job I applied for! Can you believe it?' I asked, eagerly.

'That's wonderful, dear, we'll pick up a new suit for you while we're out. So, sweetheart, where shall we start? Oxford Street or Knightsbridge?' She had a sort of vacant glare on her face.

'Are you upset about something?' I asked, timidly.

'Of course not, dear! Why ever would you say that?'

'It's the expression on your face. You look sort of, um, pained.'

'Don't be silly, Sarah, that's just the Botox,' she said, matter of factly.

'The what?'

'Botox, dear. Don't look so shocked – everyone who's anyone is doing it.' At this point I think she tried to frown but I wasn't sure as the facial paralysis she had inflicted on herself just made her look like she was trying to suppress gas. 'Now, hurry up and make yourself presentable. We don't have all day, you know.' And with that my mother made it clear that I wasn't to speak of the Botox again, and my marathon Christmas-shopping day began.

We took the tube to Oxford Street and with the pedantic precision of train spotters, we examined every item on every clothes rail in every shop we came across. I found myself feeling numb, both physically and indeed mentally, so when my mother suggested we pop into Debenham's for make-overs I followed her without resistance.

Doris, my beauty consultant, was very analytical in her approach to make-up and asked me detailed questions about my beauty regime. After telling me off for going to bed with mascara on and clarifying that I couldn't really count eight glasses of blackcurrant squash as the eight glasses of water I needed to drink every day to give me younger-looking skin, she declared that she was ready, brought over a palette of eye-shadows, powders and lip-glosses and started working on my face. I tried to tell her that I'd rather she go easy on the bronzer but couldn't really talk as she kept asking me to grimace so as to aid her search for my cheekbones.

From the corner of my eye I could see my mother – she seemed to be deeply enthralled in a serious discussion on the perils of soap-based cleansers and was oblivious to the copious amount of purple eye-shadow being piled on to her eyelids.

As I sat there daydreaming on my swivelly white faux-leather chair, Doris dramatically put down her blush brush and with a very self-satisfied tone declared her work was complete. She asked if I was ready to meet the beautiful new me. 'Yes,' I said bleakly.

With that, she turned me around and before I knew it, I was face to face with a mirror and looking back at me was a cross between an attention-seeking porn star and a children's birthday clown. Doris proceeded to hand me a yellow card that listed all the products I could use to correct my beauty problems. I thanked Doris politely for her time and bought a tube of my favourite cherry lip-gloss. Then I sneaked a couple of tissues from behind the counter and started discreetly taking off the layers of pigment on my face. I looked at the orange powder on the tissue, then at the yellow list of what was wrong with me. My natural instinct, of course, was to feel deflated and defeated, but instead I heard myself giggling, happily. Somehow, that yellow list seemed insignificant in comparison to who I was and what I was achieving in my life. 'There's so much more to me than what this powder is trying to fix and this paper is trying to correct,' I thought to myself, remembering the great news I'd woken up to that morning. And with that, I tossed away the yellow card, applied my cherry lip-gloss and walked confidently across to my mother and her very purple make-over.

The truth is that taking care of ourselves by grooming our appearance can be a good way to value ourselves. Problems only arise when we look to cosmetics, or even cosmetic surgery, to provide us with something that we can only achieve from the inside out. Most of us have fallen victim to cosmetic advertisers. We've all seen a television advert for a new face cream and marvelled at the results. Or seen a new lipstick and marvelled as we are told that it actually contains liquid diamonds! Then, of course, we rush to the stores to snap up the new miracle product, only to find that, in fact, our skin still looks the same, and it looks like we've poured a plastic container of child's play glitter on our lips. Every now and then we do find a product we feel we can't live without, but on the whole the advertising spiel turns out to be just that. We don't look younger, or slimmer, and our eyelashes haven't multiplied in thickness, length and number. So why do we continue to buy into the false dreams that beauty-product manufacturers provide? Why do we find it so hard to separate fiction from reality when we see an advert in a glossy magazine, or watch a beautiful model prance across our TV screens?

Many would say that the popularity of makeup and beauty products stems from the same basic needs that drive us to plastic surgery. We don't feel young or attractive enough so we try to change this. We decide we can't live with our bodies or faces as they are, because they tell lies about us. The Greek philosopher Hesiod wrote: 'One of the first warnings to men about the deceitfulness of women is how they disguise themselves through cosmetics.'

But is that what we are doing? Are we trying to be deceitful or are we trying to tell the truth about who we are, regardless of what our bodies are saying? The wrinkles on our faces say we are ageing when actually we feel young. The fat on our bellies says we're lazy when we are really feeling active and full of life, the droopiness of our breasts says we're past it when we know we still feel sexy. We reason that our bodies speak to others about who we are and what we stand for, so if they aren't saying what we want them to, well, then we'll translate what they say by changing how we look. The sad thing for us is that we never stop to consider that the assumptions we make about how others see us are based on our expectations and not necessarily rooted in reality, that what we say and how we act give much deeper insights into who we are than the lines on our face or the fat on our thighs. Instead we reason that the way to like ourselves is to change our looks and this makes us an advertiser's dream.

There is no escape from the adverts that bombard us on a daily basis, but we can alter the effect they have on us. Bear in mind how unrealistic the claims of these adverts are. Why should we believe the advertisers of an anti-wrinkle, age-defying skin cream when the model they use has just turned eighteen? Why should we believe the makers of an anti-cellulite cream when the smooth-skinned size eight actress flaunting it probably doesn't even know what cellulite is? Why should we believe the makers of a bust-firming gel when the woman endorsing it on our TV screens has probably had a boob job? Beauty products can give our confidence a boost, but they probably won't fulfil all the promises they make us.

The beauty industry feeds on our desire to get results quickly. We don't want to have to cut our split ends off, then wait for our hair to grow back. We want a magic cream that promises to mend them. We don't want to spend hours at the gym, toning, we want a cream that will do it for us. And there's nothing wrong with going for the speedy option – after all, that's why we have dishwashers, microwaves and cars – but we need to ensure that our beauty-buying habits are healthy.

Here are some tips to help you approach cosmetics in a healthier way.

1. Have realistic expectations about what cosmetics can do. Most of us live in hope of a cream that will obliterate cellulite for ever

leaving us free to eat as much junk food as we like, but no cream has the capacity on its own, to reduce fat and toxins, and to tone skin and muscle. So make sure that your expectations are grounded in reality no matter how good the sales pitch on the box is.

2. Ask yourself what you want cosmetics to achieve for you. Are you spending an hour on your makeup every morning because you enjoy doing it and like the way it makes you look? Or are you doing it because you're dying to ask out that guy you keep seeing in Starbucks on your coffee break? If it's the former, great! Paint away! But if it's the latter, maybe you should be spending time on your flirting technique and confidence with the opposite sex, not your makeup skills.

3. Enjoy cosmetics but don't make them into something that you have to do. Have fun with beauty products – it's great to lie in a bubble bath with a mud mask on soaking away all your stress. But if you're not up for your weekly facial steam or eye mask, give it a miss, it's not the end of the world. Don't make cosmetics a chore.

4. Experiment, but know what works for you. Have fun trying on new eye-shadow and blusher, but don't feel you need to keep up with the last word in fashion. Don't become so attached to certain products that you're afraid to try something new. Remember, makeup is there to make you feel good about yourself, not to make you feel inadequate because you've become a slave to it.

5. Don't hide behind your makeup. Using beauty products to enhance your appearance is fine, but using them to hide who you really are will only confirm the negative core belief that part of you is not good enough to be seen or needs to be hidden.

For some women, makeup is like a suit of armour they put on to protect themselves from the world. We all know at least one woman who will not leave the house, whether it be to walk the dog or put the rubbish out, without full makeup. A dependency on makeup can become unhealthy. Most women feel more confident and more relaxed when they have a little makeup on. It's amazing what a lick of lip-gloss or a stroke of the mascara wand can do, in terms of making you feel ready to face the world. Many women would not feel professional if they turned up at work with messy hair and bleary eyes. And there's nothing wrong with that. Most of us want to groom in some way before we start our day.

Also, most of us enjoy the thrill of trying new products, or stacking our shopping baskets with pretty, girly smellies in gorgeous packaging. It doesn't mean we are slaves to our beauty products: it's just another way of enjoying our appearance and valuing ourselves. However, it can tip into obsession if we find we are covering our faces with makeup before we take the kids to the park, or turning up hours late for every appointment because we have been obsessing over drawing on our eyebrows at a perfect angle.

Like sex, food and wine, applying makeup and indulging in beauty products are pleasures to be enjoyed, but can become a problem if they interfere with other aspects of everyday life. As with cosmetic surgery, women who use makeup obsessively need to ask, 'Who am I really doing this for?'

Over the years, you may have built up the impression that others will laugh at you and the planet will stop revolving if you enter the world without your blusher in place. The only way to disarm these fears is to gradually begin to put them to the test. Begin by using a little less lip-gloss, and watch people's reactions. No terrified kids? No visible responses of disgust? Of course not. You will begin to see that your makeup really isn't an integral part of who you are. Keep a diary of each step you take. And gradually, you will see makeup for what it is – paint that can enhance your features, rather than a miracle potion that will erase your insecurities and keep you immune to negative social exchanges. Don't convince yourself that you need these products to survive a possible attack on your looks, use your personality, inner strength and confidence as ammunition – they're one hell of a lot stronger than any new lipstick (no matter how glossy).

Beauty Secrets

*B*y two thirty I felt as if I had run the London marathon . . . twice . . . in heels. My mother, on the other hand, was getting her second wind, sprinting up escalators as if they weren't already moving. I pleaded with her to sit down and have a coffee with me and she finally gave in when I began trailing three shops behind. When she went off to get our decaf-skinny-might-as-well-be-drinking-tap-water coffees I noticed a tall red-headed woman dressed in too much Burberry heading towards me. 'Sarah, sweetie, how are you?' she shouted from across the room. I squinted but still couldn't make out who she was until she finally got close enough to pull me towards her and give me two very quick air kisses. It was Martha, one of my mother's tennis friends.

'What are you doing here? You're looking great . . . Is that a new hair colour? Are you alone? How's your mother? She's been naughty

– cancelled our last three tennis dates. They do great coffee in here, don't they?' I wasn't sure if she really wanted me to answer her questions so I just smiled and nodded towards my mother. 'Ah, there she is! Florence, darling, yoo-hoo!' My mother noticed her and got a slightly worried look on her face (I think) and started heading over quickly with the coffees. 'Doesn't she look great? Wow, if I didn't know better I'd say she's had something done.'

'Well, actually—' I began, when my mother darted in front of me and squealed, 'Martha, daahling how nice to bump into you like this.'

'I was just saying to Sarah that you're looking ever so well, dear. Any little secrets you'd like to share with the rest of us?'

'Oh, you know, just the usual healthy eating and exercise – does wonders you know,' my mother said, giggling nervously.

'Well, whatever it is, keep it up, it's working for you. Must dash, darling, I'm off to have tea with Jean from the club. She's just had her forehead done. Apparently she went to a different doctor this time after that fiasco with her lip injections.' She laughed with satis-faction, waved goodbye and left.

My mother turned to me almost immediately and whisper-shouted, 'You didn't say anything about the Botox, did you?'

'No, but why are you so worried? You said everyone who's anyone is doing it.'

'Well, they are, but they aren't going around telling everyone else!'
'Why not?'

'What a stupid question, Sarah! They don't talk about it because it makes it look like you're cheating not to mention that you're trying too hard . . . Beauty should be effortless.' And with that, she took out a pen, a notepad and her calorie-counter, and began trying to estimate how much of her carrot cake she could eat without exceeding her calorie limit.

I giggled at the irony of it all, and was happy that I was able to effortlessly tuck into my low-fat cherry muffin guilt free . . .

The biggest myth that women buy into is that beauty should be effortless. 'She was just born beautiful,' we say, cursing our own need to pluck hairs, conceal pimples and tone bums. We feel that beauty only counts if it's 'natural', if we can roll out of bed in the morning with glossy hair, perfect skin and sparkling teeth. To give the illusion of being naturally beautiful we spend ages in front of the mirror putting makeup on so it looks as if we aren't wearing any. And all this because we want to look beautiful, but we don't want anyone to know the lengths we go to to achieve it. Much of this secrecy is drawn from the world of advertising where deceit is part of the business. Because we believe that the twenty-something, professionally made-up, professionally photographed, professionally air-brushed model advertising wrinkle cream is a natural image, we aspire to it and, more to the point, we aspire to achieve it as naturally as it's portrayed because then it has more value. That's perhaps why some women attach a certain stigma to women whom they know or suspect have had surgery – it's seen as cheating. And when women 'cheat' and are caught out, they become a laughing-stock. The British actress Leslie Ash was teased mercilessly by national tabloids after a rather enthusiastic set of lip implants. The press was delighted at catching out a woman who decided that nature did not give her enough. As discussed earlier, women are instinctively competitive with one another, especially over appearance. Because we compete on the basis of looks with other women, when we hear that another woman has had a little help, we feel as though she's not playing fairly.

Everybody has played Spot the Boob Job or laughed at a too-tight facelift; the knowledge that another woman has had to pay for her assets makes us feel better: 'Her boobs are bigger, firmer and rounder than mine,' we reason, 'but at least mine are real.' Cosmetics and cosmetic procedures shouldn't be seen as a secret weapon in the fight against other women. If anyone's needs or agenda other than your own come into the equation when you decide on any beauty treatment from a facial to plastic surgery then it's probably not a good idea to go ahead with it.

Under the Knife

People have always been prepared to go through painful procedures to achieve a body ideal. In ancient Chinese civilisation, women strapped their toes to the soles of their feet, to conform to a torturous custom, imposed by male rulers. Eventually, the bones of the toe would snap, and the foot would cease to grow. And from this bone-crunching horror to the bashing, bruising and slicing that thousands of women put themselves through in today's world, right up to complex cosmetic surgery. Most women have strapped six-inch virtual stilts to their feet only to appear the next day with aches, pains and plasters. Most women have waxed and plucked themselves in the quest for a hair-free body. But what makes some of us go a step further and put our beauty in the hands of a surgeon? Can these operations really make a difference? And what should we ask ourselves first before we go for the chop, nip or tuck?

We tend to think of plastic surgery as a twentieth-century phenomenon, but it has been commonplace long before Pamela Anderson got us all confused between her breasts and beachballs. As early as 1000 BC, people were popping along to the nearest clinic for a nose job. Well, almost. The first plastic surgery was reported in India, where individuals who had had their noses cut off as punishment could have them reconstructed. However, plastic surgery as it is now, really caught on in the 1950s. And it's easy to see why. For those who don't subscribe to the be-happy-with-what-you're-given school of thought, it seems like a miracle cure (if a costly one, with the cheapest operations starting at about £2,500). None of that learning to accept your wonky nose or chunky thighs – you could just fix them.

The medical profession has dreamed up many weird and wonderful ways to restructure our appearance. BUPA, one of the largest health-insurance providers in Europe, estimates that in 2002 over 75,000 plastic-surgery operations were performed in the UK. The International Society of Aesthetic Plastic Surgery's (IPAS) statistics for 2000 show that the most popular forms of cosmetic alteration are, in order, liposuction and liposculpture, which involve removing or restructuring fatty areas, breast augmentation, then Botox injections, to smooth skin and 'fill out' wrinkles. Originally used for patients with facial tics, the makers realised that Botulinum toxin also ironed out wrinkles, and so began a cosmetic phenomenon. Currently the fastest growing cosmetic medical procedure in the USA, more than a million people succumbed to the 'magic' injections in 2001. According to the BBC in March 2002, sales of Botox are expected to reach $1 billion by 2006. In fact, its popularity is such that women hold 'Botox parties' at which the guest all have their faces made wrinkle-free, smooth and taut. And if a Botox party doesn't sound excessive enough, in September 2003 a well-known, London-based cosmetic-surgery practice actually launched a loyalty card. For every four visits, loyal clients are rewarded with a free non-surgical treatment, such as Botox injections. This follows the controversial cosmetic-surgery gift tokens sold by the same practice. Now, there's a body-image battering ram if ever there was one. Imagine opening your gifts on your birthday and discovering that some kind soul thinks the perfect present for you is a new nose. Charming.

The popularity of these procedures can be linked directly to our society's values. We know that it admires youth, and big breasts on a small, slender frame. Most of us realise that eternal youth and matching the body of a small girl with the bosom of a voluptuous opera singer is biologically impossible. But surgery can provide us with the assets that Mother Nature never intended. The most popular procedures focus on sexual aspects of the human body. It is far more likely that a woman will have her lips enhanced than her elbows or earlobes.

For many people, plastic surgery is about becoming more appealing to others. But does it work? Often, the success or failure of plastic surgery is directly linked to the validity of the reasons for having it in the first place. If a patient flings themselves on to the operating table, convinced that they will walk out a new person, straight into the arms of the love of their life, they are likely to see the operation as a failure. Realistically, surgery can never fulfil that dream. A flat chest won't stop you meeting 'the one', but if you feel insecure about it, it might. And while operating on their breasts may improve the confidence of some, for many others it won't take away the insecurity they feel about their bodies. In many cases, after surgery to fix one part of the body, the insecurity moves to another. That's why most of us need to operate on the insecurity rather than the lumps of fat on our chests or bottoms.

Time is the test of how successful surgery has been. A happy patient will feel satisfied with it and move on, pleased that they have been able to modify a small part of their body that they were unhappy with. But many people continue to go under the knife in a bid for perfection, they never feel content with their bodies. Someone with a negative body image may feel let down and disappointed with the result because it doesn't make them feel more confident. Their thighs may be slimmer, but they still feel unhappy and self-conscious about their body. They reason, 'Yes, my thighs look better, but I still feel ugly, so it must be my nose. I'll have a nose job.' And so begins a spiral of plastic surgery addiction. If you refuse to look at the real reason for your insecurities then chances are you will keep going under the knife, desperately trying to solve the problems externally.

When therapists work with patients who have suffered serious disfigurements, they try to establish a point at which a patient will accept that surgery has played its part, and that now they must rebuild their confidence from the inside. To a lesser degree, this can also be true of people having surgery for cosmetic reasons. We need to know where to draw the line. For as long as people are prepared to pay for plastic surgery, surgeons will dream up new ways to work on our bodies. In America the latest trend is cosmetic foot surgery: toes are filed down and fat is sliced off so that the patient can wear the latest strappy sandals, and so another, some would argue unnecessary, surgery trend begins. There will always be somebody willing to promise you the perfect body, for a (not so) small fee.

But no matter how wonderful the surgeon, true self-esteem and confidence come from within, which is why it's important to grasp that at some point you will need to work on your internal feelings. And it's easy to see why women put that off for so long. After all, it's far simpler to dissect and rebuild a not-so-perfect nose than it is to rebuild an unhealthy body image. And unless we are prepared to acknowledge that our motivation in undergoing cosmetic surgery is not merely a product of our judgements about how our body looks but how we think and feel about the role that our appearance plays in our life, we aren't being honest about why we are choosing to change our bodies.

Demedicalising Surgery

*A*t five fifteen we had finally moved into the male gift-buying portion of the day. As we pondered nasal hair-clippers and solar-powered flashlights for my father, my mother brought up the subject of her Botox again. 'So, Sarah dear, as I was saying earlier, the doctor who did my face is absolutely wonderful – I mean the results do speak for themselves,' she said smugly, picking up a novelty mirror that shouted, 'You're a babe!' when you squeezed its handle. She smiled modestly as though genuinely touched by the computerised compliment and continued. 'Listen, dear, the doctor who did it was just wonderful, in fact I spoke to him about you and your, er, difficulty in adhering to diets. He said he has a great new technique for liposuction that might work for you.'

I ignored her and tried to change the subject. 'How about a wok? Dad likes Chinese food, let's get him a wok.'

'No, dear, he'll make a mess in the kitchen and besides Chinese food gives him trapped wind; let's stick to the non-foodie gadgets. Now, as I was saying, this lovely doctor has a gift-voucher scheme so, I was thinking, we still haven't got your Christmas present and, *well, I know it's a little pricey but if you're a very good girl maybe Santa will be extra generous this year . . .'*

I genuinely couldn't believe my ears. My mother was actually suggesting buying me plastic surgery as a stocking filler. I was totally lost for words. All of a sudden I could feel that the way I looked or, more importantly, the way I didn't look, was becoming once again the centre of my attention. My mother, completely oblivious to the effect of her perverse gift idea, happily continued rummaging through wood-carving sets and stamp collecting albums. I picked up the novelty mirror she had looked into earlier. As I gazed at the face staring back at me, it occurred to me that cosmetic surgery, like the makeup, the clothes and diets, was a prop. Stuff to hide behind to make you feel safer. In a lot of ways they were good things, making you feel that little bit better about your looks. But none of it had the ability by itself to make me feel better or worse about myself. Rather, all these things acted like security blankets, allowing people to feel more in control in the world of beauty – a world so unpredictable and so confused that any trend, no matter how popular, is over within a few months. For the first time in a long time, I felt like I got it . . . it wasn't about what I believed but rather what I chose to believe. Well, Sarah, I thought, I choose to believe that you're OK without the orange powder and ridiculous gift vouchers. Whether you're eating chocolate or drinking decaf, wearing a smock or a bikini, the one constant thing, the one certain thing is you . . . the real you.

And in that instant I actually felt more in control of my life than I ever had before. 'You're a babe!' shouted the gimmicky mirror, right on cue. I giggled, kissed my mother and told her I had to run, then darted out of the shop and raced home, thinking that at last I was ready to ask James out.

We live in a culture that demands fast results. If we go to a fast-food chain we want our burger quickly. If we want to lose weight, we know we should exercise and eat three good meals a day, but we crash-diet because we want people to notice the change tomorrow when we go to work. Plastic surgery is an extension of this. We can have Botox injections in the lunch hour, or collagen implants before the kids have to be picked up from school. And, more dramatically, we can have our chests pumped with silicone and appear two weeks later with the boobs we've always dreamt of. People have even started jetting off to the Mediterranean on plastic-surgery holidays.

This trend doesn't only have consequences for the 'quick fix' culture but is a step towards demedicalising a major form of surgery. Every year thousands of tourists flock to South Africa, taking full advantage of the currency exchange rate and, consequently, cheap cosmetic surgery. Bringing home a tan and a pair of castanets is now a little *passé*. Serious tourists bring back slimmer hips, straighter noses and bigger boobs. Surgeons in Cape Town organise packages including the operation itself, and rest and recuperation facilities. A quick search on the Internet reveals a number of companies offering sun, sea, sand and scalpel – for example, 'Surgeon and Safari'. Combining a holiday with a plastic-surgery procedure makes it sound like a stay at a health farm, with an added extra. In fact, many women regard a trip to the plastic surgeon in the same way as an appointment with a beautician. People have their noses rebuilt as they would pop along to have their bikini lines waxed – except there's probably less pain involved.

This sets a dangerous precedent. The potential danger of anaesthesia is forgotten in the quest to look perfect. And these operations do have the potential to go wrong. Implants leak, wrinkles reappear and lifts sag. In 2003

America's Food and Drug Administration pointed out that four in ten people who take the Botox path to everlasting youth suffer some sort of side effect, including drooping eyelids, nausea and even respiratory infections. If you travel abroad to place yourself under a surgeon's knife there are added dangers, such as the lack of aftercare, and an increased risk of deep-vein thrombosis on the flight back. It's also a little harder to storm into your surgeon's office and demand a refund if it all goes wrong when he's on the other side of the world.

Botox parties, plastic holidays and gift vouchers demedicalise what really are serious procedures, and allow us to lull ourselves into a false sense of security. It is essential that the health implications of plastic surgery are not submerged in gift vouchers, coffee mornings or holidays abroad. Cosmetic surgery is all too often seen as a quick fix, and that couldn't be further from the truth.

Surgery and Identity

The International Association of Plastic Surgeons found that 87 per cent of its patients were women. Either men are less inclined to 'change' their bodies because they are less worried about the way they look, or they feel plastic surgery is a female way to deal with body dissatisfaction.

Some research suggests that successful plastic surgery can act as a catalyst for a better relationship with your body, but there is also evidence that although one may feel better about the feature that was operated on, body image as a whole does not improve.

Do we go under the knife to look beautiful or just better?

And who has the most impact on our decision? Ourselves, our partners, our friends, the surgeon? A recent study looked at women in the Netherlands who had undergone surgery. In Holland, cosmetic surgery is free to any woman who can prove their body is falling 'outside the realm of the normal'. Therefore, financial pressures are less important. Researchers found that the women interviewed were not simply slaves to the beauty myth. Rather, they saw surgery as a last resort after struggling to feel normal or accepted. Also, these women felt that the surgery would help them gain control of their bodies; it was not a way to please their partners or to banish any other pressure. Consequently the authors of the study see cosmetic surgery as a way to modify identity so that women feel they 'fit' into their body and are comfortable with it. Interestingly, when people undergo gender assignment operations because they feel they were 'born in the wrong body', society can be understanding, empathising with the dilemma of feeling 'out of place' in one's own body. Women who have cosmetic surgery, on the other hand, are often seen as vain lemmings, controlled by society's body ideals. The authors of the study argue that for these women, plastic surgery served the same purpose, namely to align identity with their bodies, so that they can feel comfortable with them.

This stands as one explanation for why hundreds of women allow surgeons to cut and paste their bodies each year. Perhaps in our minds we see our ideal bodies in a certain way, and cosmetic surgery can change our appearance so that it matches the image. Therefore if the motivation is to move closer to a personal ideal, then cosmetic surgery can be seen as an assertion of control, rather than submission. Not surprisingly, this point of view is strongly contested by other researchers, who argue that we need to ask where the idealised notions of beauty come from.

It has been argued that such an idealised image is the result of society's imposed ideals of what one has to look like in order to be accepted – a reaction to faulty core beliefs. Others assert that plastic surgery is just a way of conforming to beauty ideals that are ultimately created by men, even if women feel they are making their own choice, it has in fact been made for them by friends and partners, and supported by the medical profession. Women's magazines carry endless photographs of perfect models alongside advertisements for cosmetic surgery. The media paints a picture of plastic surgery as acceptable and, indeed, desirable. Women may simply be giving in blindly to these pressures, reinforcing dominant male ideologies.

There is no simple answer as to whether the decision to undergo a surgical procedure to improve appearance is a good or bad one, and frankly, making it a moral issue is wrong – women have enough guilt and pressure to contend with in every other aspect of their lives. However, if we are contemplating surgery, we can and should look at the facts surrounding how our body image feeds the decision. It is imperative that we take on board that our body image, as opposed to our actual body, has a profound effect on the way we see ourselves. Any attempt to improve the way we look should begin with a thorough examination of why we see what we see when we look in the mirror, and how to address perceptions that make us feel uncomfortable with our appearance. Our core beliefs are constantly being bombarded with the message that we should try to attain the perfect appearance, but the only way we can begin to challenge the stereotypical notions that dictate who we should be is by taking a good look at the reasons behind our actions, and by acknowledging that, in most cases, the ideal 'you' that you have in your mind was not your idea in the first place.

Now, for those who have done the soul-searching and are seriously considering plastic surgery, here are some important questions to ask yourself before you make your final decision.

1. Why do I want this surgery?

The answer to this question should either ring warning bells, or comprehensively justify the surgery. For example, if the answer is 'Well, big bottoms are really fashionable this year,' then perhaps you should think again. This is where you must be honest with yourself. While you might be telling friends that you want liposuction to 'feel healthier', deep down you'll know if it is to bring a cheating husband to heel, or help you compete with your younger sister.

2. What do I expect from this surgery?

If you think that the surgery will land you the perfect job or boyfriend, chances are you'll be disappointed. Look at the surgery realistically. It might boost your confidence, but it won't bring you all the things you feel you lack, unless your body image is healthy enough to allow you to see realistically the results of the surgery. Even if plastic surgery gets you the firmest thighs in the world, it won't make much difference if your core beliefs are irrational. They need to be healthy enough for you to acknowledge that your thighs, no matter how firm, will not make people love and accept you. Your personality, self-esteem and confidence will dictate that.

3. Whose life will the surgery change?

What implications does the surgery have for those around you? And how healthy is their impact on your decision? There are some reasons why plastic surgery can be a good idea. That your husband loves big boobs is not one of them. This question is really to do with approval-seeking. Do you feel that your family will accept you better and that you will all be closer if you have a cute little button nose just like theirs rather than the one you were born with? Perhaps you want to fit in with the skinny girls at work. Perhaps you're a guy who thinks a face-lift will help him blend in among his younger team-mates after Wednesday-night football. Why do you think these people can't accept you? Why do you *assume* or *imagine* that they don't accept you? Perhaps you are not accepting yourself. As with any aspect of body image, the key is to accept what you look like, and then be realistic about the influence it has on your successes or failures in life. If you have an operation for anyone other than yourself, you probably won't fulfil your aim because the key to pleasing that person will not be sucking fat out of your bum and injecting it into your face. How fair are that person's expectations of you? If you judge them to be irrational, ask yourself if you should be listening to or affected by them.

4. How will it affect my relationships?

Sometimes our desire for surgery goes far deeper than wanting a straighter nose or a bigger bust. Sometimes we expect it to have massive implications for our relationships. A man may long for a penis enlargement because he feels inadequate in his relationship, and blames the perceived inadequacy for every fight he has with his girlfriend. Or a woman might feel that her husband would be more attentive if she had bigger breasts. So we go under the knife to make improvements to our relationships. There are two possible outcomes. Your relationship may improve because you feel more confident and happy within yourself. But if you have plastic surgery to save a failing relationship, you may reveal your new breasts to a disappointing reaction. The absence of whoops of joy, a marriage proposal and endless attention will make you feel pretty low if they were your main goals in having the operation. If you have a penis enlargement and find that your girlfriend becomes obsessed with what's going on in your trousers, and is just a little *too* pleased, you might question how bad the situation was before, or wonder why she's in a relationship with you in the first place. If we base our desire for plastic surgery on our relationship, then we need to be prepared for unpredictable and often disappointing results.

5. What is the ideal I am striving for?

Again, we need to be realistic. If we want to be the first human Barbie doll, it will probably take more than a minor nip or tuck. And you need to ask why you're striving for this ideal. Do you feel you should have a slimmer tummy because other people are judging you? And who's making the decision? You or the pressures around you? People have always felt pressured by society's values. That's why women squeezed and squealed their way into corsets and why men spend hours pumping whatever they pump at the gym. One of the easiest ways of understanding society's ideals is to look at the stars of the time. Twiggy, Marilyn Monroe, Kate Moss and Jennifer Lopez have all enjoyed stints as body role models. And they all have very different bodies. So, the chances are that if you are striving to look like J-Lo's twin sister, then you're going to look very out of fashion when a new body drifts into the public eye. And not many people can afford to check into a cosmetic-surgery clinic every time *Vogue* has a new cover girl. The ideal you should be aiming for is a body that will enable you to feel the best you can feel, not to look like the hottest star of the moment.

Time Stands Still For No One . . .

Miracle face creams, heavy makeup and plastic surgery are all a response to feelings of inadequacy about our body, especially with regard to the ageing process. As we get older and realise that our body is liable to wrinkle, sag and weaken, we may feel as if we're losing control of it. Consequently, we alter our bodies to feel more in control. In puberty changes to our body mean we become stronger, more capable and more attractive to the opposite sex. Later in life, the body deteriorates and we have to come to terms with the revelation that there is nothing we can do about it.

The ageing process can be particularly hard for women. The realisation that we can no longer command the same attention from men can be a hard pill to swallow. However, the key to dealing with this is to understand that the ageing process and factors such as the menopause have no effect on our genuine appeal to others. Women are not sexy because they menstruate regularly, what makes us attractive is confidence, self-belief and positive personality traits such as a sense of humour. These qualities linger far longer than a pert set of boobs or a glossy mane of dark hair. Also, it's important that as our time as a sex kitten passes, we focus on other assets to make us feel good about ourselves. Taking up hobbies such as yoga or swimming can help us to use our body in new ways. Taking up art, or photography, or any number of pastimes can help us define ourselves as women, rather than sex objects, and appreciate that while our bodies may now fail to attract the wolf-whistles of passing guys, it can help us achieve new, more satisfying goals. This, in turn, reminds us to respect our body, rather than blame it for entirely natural changes.

It is important to confront insecurities about ageing with your partner. Much of body image is about the way we feel others see us. Because we find ourselves less attractive due to grey hair or wrinkled skin, we assume that our partner feels the same. He's never commented on it, but we assume it anyway. But there are a thousand things that our partners find attractive about us, and minor physical details, such as smooth eyelids, probably come pretty low on the list. They probably haven't noticed the things that we imagine dominate our appearance. If you keep open the lines of communication between you, your partner can tell you how ridiculous you're being when you confront him with your body concerns. Often we only need a nudge of reassurance from those who mean most to us.

If beauty led to happiness, then all good-looking people would be blissfully happy all the time and all unattractive people would be miserable. Doctors would prescribe surgery and makeup instead of anti-depressants. Of course this isn't the case. Good-looking people suffer from body-image and eating disorders as much as less attractive people; and some of the most successful, confident, happy people in the world are far from being classically beautiful. Beauty does not make us immune to unhappiness. What does help is high self-esteem, a positive body image and the confidence to deal with what life throws at you. Beauty products, makeup and surgery can all be a great way to improve how we feel about ourselves, if we use them for the right reasons – that means doing it for ourselves and nobody else. It means having realistic expectations of what we hope for from the face cream, blusher or liposuction. And it means accepting that, in the end, the key to achieving the body of the moment probably won't unlock the solution to our biggest problems. Many people realise this too late, once they've spent fortunes on cosmetic miracles or even gone under the knife and they discover that although their looks have changed, everything else is pretty much the same.

Everybody wants the quick fix, and cosmetic surgery can be a great way to achieve results fast. But before you book in for a weekly facial or an operation that will require you to remortgage your house, make sure you know what you expect to change when you emerge afterwards. It's easy to load all our insecurities on to one body part and blame it for every unhappy aspect of our life. But no face cream or surgeon can change a poor body image, which is often the only beauty treatment we need. It's a hell of a lot cheaper too.

TAKE AWAYS

For many people, makeup and plastic surgery seem like a simple route to fixing body-image problems – but, as this chapter has shown, a change to your body doesn't guarantee that your body image will change with it. At best changing your appearance can make you look at yourself differently, the beginning of the journey to body satisfaction; at worst it can displace the discontent you feel about one body part to another. Like most things to do with body image, cosmetics and cosmetic surgery are neither good nor bad. The only thing that gives them value is what we expect of them. In these exercises we'll examine some of the expectations we have of our bodies, and also learn to value them in ways that don't involve what we see in the mirror.

TASK 1

This is one of my favourites. It's about making amends with your body – doing something nice for it. Really, you've spent so long being angry with it and criticising it that now it's time to make peace. Take a long bubble bath, buy yourself a professional massage or give yourself a manicure. Maybe you feel good when you're doing something active: go swimming, dancing, riding. While you're doing these things focus on how your body *feels* and make a point of noting the positive feelings associated with taking care of yourself. When you have completed your 'feel good' exercise, stand in front of the mirror and tell yourself what you like about your body. No matter how silly you feel, try to do this because it really does work. Focus on valuing yourself, remember the pleasure you had when you did your 'feel good' exercise and acknowledge that your body can make you feel great.

TASK 2

By now you must be an expert at relaxation and positive imagery. This is an extension of that exercise. Lie down and do the deep relaxation exercise (see page 130), but this time as you focus on each part of your body describe something that you like about it, in terms of how it looks and how it feels. From your toes to the top of your head, value each and every part of you.

TASK 3

This task is simple but effective and you should try to do it every time you look into the mirror, whether it's to tidy your hair in the morning or to try on a new dress in a shop. Make a point of finding something you like about your appearance. We spend so much time focusing on things we don't like when we look into the mirror that we forget to value ourselves. If we make a point of finding something positive about our appearance, we grind down the negative beliefs that tell us we are the sum total of our flaws. We begin to see our bodies in a more positive, healthy light, which confirms that we like the person in the mirror.

Chapter Eight

YOUR MIRROR

Wow! I can't believe it! I'm actually going to ask James out. After months of pining for him I'm really going to do it. Am going to look so fab walking into Bea's wedding with him on my arm. OK . . . what to wear? Am definitely wearing favourite uber-sexy black lace knickers. Every time I walk past a man with these on I think, 'You want me and you don't even know it.' OK, boobs are my favourite part of me so will wear top that subtly yet obviously reveals my cleavage – any of Aunt Cecilia's recent gifts will do, really . . . ah, there it is, the lilac sweater she gave me last Christmas. OK, will wear the black trousers I bought last week with Antonio and fab new ankle boots with killer heel. Right, extra attention to makeup today. I will clean off last night's mascara before I put on a new layer this morning . . . great, a little cherry lip-gloss and I'm done. Final check in full-length mirror. I begin focussing on my boots, not bad – very sexy and S&M, even though I got them in the sale at M&S. Trousers looking fine – my bum still not my favourite part of me, but hey, if I don't focus on it then maybe no one else will. Top looks fab, must say, love my boobs – perky but in a healthy Finnish milk-maid way rather than a page-3 girl sort of way. Right, makeup's looking good, hair needs a bit more serum, a bit less pouffiness . . . that's it. OK I'm ready . . .

As I pick up my coat and bag to head out of the door, I feel as if I'm forgetting something . . . something's missing. I turn around and go back to my room, switch on the light and look in the mirror.

*I look at the body staring back at me and feel I owe it an apology.
I feel strange but I start to speak: 'Listen, I know we've had some
rough times, you and me, but I just want you to know that even
though I criticise you and call you names and even hate parts of you,
that really I don't mean it. I like you – I like me – and I appreciate
the way you make me feel and the things I can do because of you.
Listen, let's call a truce – I mean, I understand that you've got a
screwed-up sense of humour and that you'll still throw the odd
surprise pimple at me when I least expect it, but if I stop slagging
you off as much as I do and blaming you for everything in my life,
can we agree to be a little nicer to each other' and, well, eventually
accept and love each other? 'OK, cool. You're looking great, babe.'
I wink at myself. 'Good luck!' And with that, I leave my flat feeling
better about myself than I have in a very long time.*

Wow! Here we are at the last chapter. Take a moment to
congratulate yourself. Finding the conviction to explore
and confront those thoughts and beliefs that have been part
of your life for so long is not easy. It takes courage. It takes
faith in yourself and in the notion that things can change.
Having made the journey this far, you'll have begun to feel
better about yourself and, of course, your body image.
You'll have learnt that what matters in life is not what you
see but the way you see it, and that you can only begin to
value your body when you start valuing the person inside.

From identifying and challenging negative assumptions
to learning deep relaxation techniques and guided imagery to face your own worst-case scenarios, you have
achieved a lot. You have started a process through which
you have learnt to challenge your worldview and replace it
with a healthier one. The time and effort you've invested
will ensure that you're able to cope with challenges you'll

face in the future. No doubt there will be some days when you feel better about your appearance than others, and that's fine, as long as you don't forget that the real culprit is not what is going on in your mirror but, rather, what's going on in your head.

Remember, better body image is a lifestyle change, so an important part of maintaining the gains you've made is to continue with the exercises and challenging your thoughts to avoid falling back into old, unhelpful patterns of negative thinking. Now that you're investing in yourself and improving your body image it's important to keep up the good work. Unless you practise you'll forget the important lessons that you've learnt about yourself and your body image. It's vital to keep up with the skills, and exercises, and, as much as you can, apply them to your daily life. The more you do this the more it will become an effortless part of your everyday life. Some days will, of course, seem easier than others, but it's on these difficult days that you will need to remind yourself that it's normal to feel down sometimes, we all have bad-hair days, and with the skills you've learnt you will be able to cope with any bad-hair day (no matter how frizzy). So, go forward armed with the knowledge that there is more to you than what you see in the mirror.

By learning to identify and challenge negative beliefs about your appearance you have achieved something really wonderful. You have taken control of your body image, rather than allowing your negative perceptions to dictate how you see yourself and the world around you. In developing a better body image you have banished the mental limitations that were holding you back, and you've allowed yourself the freedom to embrace life on your terms. Now anything is possible. You can achieve all those things you've dreamt of because there is nothing to stop you. Now, the one calling the shots is you. Not the *have-tos* and *shoulds* that dictated how you lived your life for so long, but you, the real you.

Seeking to control our lives through our appearance is futile, because appearance is just the way you look, not who you are, what you stand for or believe in. Keep things in perspective: enjoy cool clothes and sparkly lip-gloss, if they make you feel good about yourself, but learn to feel good about yourself regardless of them. And next time you find yourself in front of a mirror instead of asking, 'Mirror, mirror, on the wall, who's the fairest of them all?' tell yourself that no mirror or indeed no reflection from anyone or anything defines you – you are beautiful because of who you are and no one has the power to tell you otherwise.

Here are some points to keep in mind as you begin your life with a better body image.

1. First you think . . . then you feel

This is probably one of the most important lessons to take away from this book. Nothing in this life is stressful or anxiety-provoking or bad or good. It's all about how we see or make sense of an experience that gives it meaning. We are confronted with a situation, we assess it, make sense of it, and then we have an emotional reaction to it. When you look in the mirror you focus on what you don't like and contemplate how your dreaded Roman nose or frizzy hair will ruin your life. This will lead you to feel upset and to lose confidence in yourself, which will affect every inter-action that you have for the rest of the day. Alternatively, you can reason that these features are not so bad, that they make you an individual, that there is so much more to you than your nose or hair or any other part of your body for that matter. And so move on to focus on what you do like about yourself. This will lead you to feel more positive about yourself, to see who you are and what you have to offer in broader terms than just appearance. Consequently this type of thinking will have a positive impact on the way you relate to others and on your life. It's simple to remember and, once you get used to it, not so hard to do. Soon you'll find that you're correcting your negative thinking without even being conscious of it, and that's a huge part of having a better body image.

2. Mirrors reflect more than you see

Imagine if there were no such things as mirrors. We'd have to judge how we look by how we feel. We'd have to believe other people when they told us we looked great. And, most importantly, we'd probably have about an hour extra each day. Mirrors allow us to assess ourselves, and – depending on our mood, the experiences we have been through and the impact of our environment – throw up glowing or damning reports. When we look in a mirror, we see a reflection of our appearance and of all our hopes, fears and insecurities. What we do not see is an accurate representation of what we look like. We see emotions, feelings and memories. We look in a mirror and see the fat girl who was teased at school. Or perhaps we see a sex kitten who's just been asked for a date by the hot guy she sits next to on the bus every morning.

Sometimes we feel great about our appearance, sometimes we feel bad, and sometimes, well, it just doesn't seem important. It's up to you what you choose to see when you look at yourself in the mirror. You choose to focus on the negatives or the positives, to see what either a bully or a loved one sees. You just need to use the tools you've learnt to see the person you are.

3. Core beliefs shape our perspective and perspective is everything

Core beliefs develop early on in life and serve as tinted glasses that colour the way we see things. Being aware of our core beliefs, of what colour glasses we are wearing, will give us a clearer picture of how we see things. Remember, one of the biggest steps in moving towards a better body image is exploring the core beliefs that sustain it. They serve as the foundation for all the negative and irrational thinking that underpins the negative feelings you have towards your body. Working towards a better body image means identifying and understanding your core beliefs and using this knowledge to make sense of the way you see and interact with your body. Remember, you have learnt how to put things into a better perspective, to challenge the negative thoughts derived from unhelpful core beliefs. Putting things into perspective helps us see how irrational many of our body fears are.

Cognitive therapy is all about testing fears and putting them into proportion. It seems ironic that so many people hold down steady jobs, run happy families and live their lives by a series of practical, well-judged decisions, yet when it comes to their own body they are incapable of seeing things for what they are. A successful managing director may be consumed by anxiety about his greying hair. A bright, happy, popular schoolgirl might be obsessed with the gap between her front teeth. Understand that you are probably overestimating the importance of a 'flaw', that the colour of your hair or the gap between your teeth isn't the cause of your life worries. We blame our appearance because it is the most obvious thing about us. When we look into a mirror, we can't see intelligence, warmth or kindness, but we can see the big red spot. It is also easier to blame our appearance for our failures because it seems easier to change than anything else. Body image is not a physical concept, so taking physical measures to remedy a negative body image probably won't work.

4. The world does not revolve around your bum (or any other part of your body for that matter)

It's easy to assume that strangers will feel as we do about our appearance. But in most cases they won't notice the little things that drive us into a cold sweat. It's irrational to assume that everyone in a group of people is thinking about your fat thighs. No, they're thinking about their dinner tonight, or stresses at work, or even their own fat thighs. Healthy body image is about thinking realistically, and the reality is that no one pays as much attention to your body imperfections as you do. Wolf-whistlers, playground bullies and sleazy men in bars will come and go, but if you feel positive about your body they won't bother you.

5. Learn to accept you

Try to accept that we never have much control over our bodies. The sooner we accept it, the easier it is. Because the other option is starting down a path of self-hatred and continuous dissatisfaction, where we single out something we dislike about ourselves and then generalise this criticism using it as an overall description of who we are. Eventually we feel resentful towards an offending body part and extend this criticism to ourselves until we reject who we are. We fail to see ourselves realistically, and realism is vital in establishing a healthy body image. It may be easier to blame a problem or failure on a physical trait that we have no control over but it's far more satisfying and confidence-boosting to establish where you're going wrong, and to remedy it; it also helps you to see that your appearance was probably irrelevant. Again, it's about putting it all in perspective.

6. Learn to ask yourself what the worst-case scenario is

If you feel like you are never going to form a lasting relationship with someone really special, get the job or make a new friend then the results can't get much worse. But they could be a whole lot better. Take your anxieties to their worst possible conclusion. What is the worst thing that can happen if you approach that fantastic guy and ask him out for dinner? The world won't stop revolving, you won't stop breathing, and the ground won't open up and swallow you, even if at that particular moment it sounds like an appealing option. The worst that can happen is that he says, 'No.' It's only a word. It can't hurt you that much.

And he might refuse you on the basis of looks, but if he does, do you really want to go out for dinner with him anyway? How deep will a relationship be if it involves someone who judges people on their looks? About as deep as a day-old puddle. (For non-puddle experts, that's not very deep.) More likely, if he refuses it will be for another reason, entirely unrelated to your big feet or spotty chin. Shrug it off, and move on. He may, of course, say, 'Yes.' He might just take you up on your offer. He may have seen your warmth, kindness and sense of humour rather than your big feet. And after that? The dinner may be cold, the conversation may be sparse and you may never see him again. But at least you'll have the confidence boost firmly under your belt. You'll know what it feels like to take a risk and come off as a winner. You'll know that you can make your personality your most attractive feature, and that next time it'll be a whole lot easier.

7. Body image will grow and develop as you do

There are a number of life processes that everyone goes through that will influence body image, from early child-hood, when we first understand that our body can be seen negatively or positively, to adolescence, when our body is changing at a rate beyond our control, to adulthood and ageing where our identity is bound up in the way we look. Our body image evolves with us, allowing us to make sense of our world and our place within it – but all the time underscoring the reality that no matter what stage of life we are at, the actual input we have in the way we look is fairly limited. What we can control is our acceptance and ability to cope with it. Nothing your body does, whether that be gaining a stone in weight, or developing a family of pimples on your forehead, is that scary, unless we let it become so. The key to developing a healthy body image is challenging our negative or irrational thoughts and looking at ourselves as individuals rather than just body parts – from adolescence right through to old age.

8. You can't change the past but you can influence the future

Most of us have had experiences we'd rather forget. But whether it was name-calling in the playground or being compared to a prettier younger sister in adolescence, such experiences make up part of our personal history. More importantly, however, the way we let them affect us makes up who we are and how we behave in the present. We are not slaves to our past because, no matter how traumatic, we all have the capacity to heal and grow. Looking at past experiences may help you explain why you feel negatively about your body image but it won't help you resolve it – if anything, focusing on the past reinforces the idea that you are helpless and unable to move forward. The only way that positive change can occur is if you take responsibility for the choices you make today. Your choices, behaviour and experiences today will make up your history tomorrow.

9. Stop using your body to hang your problems on

As the most obvious part of your identity, your body is often what you turn to in order to explain feelings of in-adequacy or despair. You can blame a multitude of sins on a big nose, short stature or bad skin. It's a simple route to justify why things didn't go your way. But the reality is that this is missing the point. If you buy into the idea that looking good is the only way to be happy, you will consistently undermine your capacity to grow and learn about yourself and inevitably feel unhappy not just about your body but about your life as a whole.

10. Stop seeking reassurance from elsewhere: learn to reassure yourself

Contrary to what some cable TV shows might tell you, most people can't read minds. When you are feeling insecure about your appearance and require reassurance from others, it's likely that they won't know it. You can (a) learn to ask for an honest opinion from your partner and friends and learn to accept compliments (as opposed to dismissing them with 'you're just saying that because you have to') or (b) learn to reassure yourself. By doing the latter you will become less approval-seeking and less likely to be focused on the way you look when you interact with others (so when they do give you a compliment it comes as a nice surprise rather than as a seal of approval).

11. You, not your looks, dictate your destiny

We are constantly bombarded with the idea that pretty people deserve and consequently get the best things in life. If you accept it, you will condemn yourself to a mediocre life and deny yourself the opportunity to learn from your mistakes: you'll attribute all your setbacks to how you look. Successful people (like unsuccessful people) come in all shapes and sizes: to define your ambitions and aspirations by your appearance is to put unnecessary obstacles in your way. Make decisions about your future based not on what you look like but on where your passions lie. Don't be afraid to follow your dreams or aspirations: they will say more about you than your height, weight or any other body feature ever could.

12. It's not just girls

For years men have relaxed in the knowledge that they don't need to worry too much about that paunchy belly or balding head because the respect and admiration they receive from others is based on the amount they earn and their achievements. Typically, men have been more likely to be judged on how attractive their partner is than how attractive they are. We've all heard a man get respect from other men in this way – 'Cor, he's done well! Look at his girlfriend!' Or words to that effect. The truth is that until recently, the term 'body image' probably sounded like a foreign language to most guys. Now, though, it is something they have to deal with in the same way as women. The Chippendales, the Dreamboys, a plethora of scantily clad boy-band hunks and a move towards equal rights have all contributed to the rise of the male body as an assessed object. Men's health magazines have alerted them to the fact that they should be exfoliating, pampering and generally taking greater interest in their appearance. While diet clubs are jam-packed with women striving (or should that be starving?) for the body beautiful, gyms are chock-a-block with men sweating it out for exactly the same reason. Of course, men have always felt a degree of body dissatisfaction, but the new prominence of rippling male bodies as

a popular and acceptable image has given them a clear idea
of how they should want to look. We've got Barbie, they've
got Action Man. So, men can be as insecure about the way
they look as women, if for different reasons. It's important to bear this in mind, because while you're worrying
that your new man will be repelled by your flabby bum,
you're completely oblivious to the fact that he will probably have a few body anxieties of his own. Sometimes,
hearing about other people's insecurities helps us put our
own into perspective.

13. Enter new relationships liking who you are

Nothing will kill off a good potential relationship quicker
than body insecurities. They act like sex-repellent unless we
can grasp how irrational most of them are. From the sparks
of a new flirtation to the day you celebrate your seventieth
wedding anniversary, the way we feel about ourselves can
have a tremendous impact on the path our relationships
take. If we feel unhappy about our looks, we won't return
the smile that the good-looking man in the pub flashes at
us: we worry about rejection, and that taking a risk will
make us feel even less attractive. And the irony is that if
our crooked nose feels like the most obvious thing about
us, and we try to hide it, it will probably *become* the most
obvious thing about us. If, however, we behave as though
it isn't a problem, it probably won't be. Especially if you
give people a hundred and one other things to notice instead.

So, approach the guy in the pub, and imagine you're
handing him your CV. At the top is your name, so introduce yourself. Now, don't let the next line read, 'crooked
nose.' Instead showcase your best qualities. You put the

most exciting things first on a CV, so do this in your life. You want him to notice your great personal qualities first, so go and put them out there. Make a joke, pay him a compliment, be a great listener. Do anything that blows your body worries out of the water. The majority of people will only notice your body problems if you give them nothing else to go on. Think of the most memorable people you know. They aren't so special to you because of how they look, are they? It might be the science teacher who inspired you to fight for your dreams. It might be your boss, who always gets her own way because she is so assertive. It might be your mother, because of the selfless charity work she does. Equally, when you first meet someone, a real fondness for them, and a great first impression comes from the way you connect with them, not how long their eyelashes are, or how straight their nose is. You will be accorded true respect and admiration for who you are, not what you look like.

14. You're in competition with no one but yourself

The problem with asking, 'Mirror, mirror on the wall, who's the fairest of them all?' is that we're signing up to a competition we can't win. Women believe they're in this 'Great Competition' and unfortunately you don't get a say in whether or not you compete. Nope, as soon as that stork drops off a little pink bundle, you're a fully paid-up competitor. Your opponents? Every other woman in your life. Average competing time? An entire lifespan. The prize? Prince Charming. Woman are taught from babyhood that their ultimate goal is to win the Great Competition. Winning involves fighting off every other woman to find the perfect man. Because from day one, women compete on the basis of looks. It's why we bitch about other women's figures, hair or makeup. It's why we feel more confident in a room full of women we think are less attractive than ourselves, and less confident when we feel we are the least attractive. Competing in this way encourages us to feel negatively about other women, and forces us to place a ridiculous amount of emphasis on the way we look.

The fact is, that the only people who control how women relate to one another are women themselves. We are exasperated when we feel we are being valued simply on the basis of our appearance, but more often than not it is the first comparison we use when competing with other women. We have been assessed in terms of attractiveness for so long that it is the only currency we use. But it's up to us to change it. Instead we should start to negotiate with qualities that have nothing to do with appearance. There will always be an element of competition in some aspects of our life, but if we must compete, let's compete with ourselves in an effort to achieve our own personal best rather than trying to emulate anyone else's records.

15. You don't have to buy what the media tells you

The media thrives on selling the beauty myth; a ridiculous degree of importance is placed on appearance and glamour; you can't escape the loaded messages about beauty coming at you from every direction. However, it is up to you how you choose to assimilate and make sense of this information. You can choose to believe that the eighteen-year-old model being used to sell wrinkle cream is a fifty-two-year-old grandmother in real life and therefore a realistic image that you should aspire to, or you can see it as a marketing ploy. You can choose to believe that everyone in the world, according to television, is a size eight or less, or you can look around you and see that the real world has little to do with TV Land. Marketing campaigns will continue to try to sell you happiness, love and confidence with featured products, but there are some things that money can't buy. Screen out the messages that tell you you are not good enough and invest in yourself, your identity, your confidence, the real you.

16. Take care of yourself inside and out

Even though good body image comes from the inside, it involves valuing yourself in any way that makes you feel good. It certainly doesn't mean abandoning all the things you do to make yourself feel attractive. You don't have to hide your hairbrush, boycott the gym and ditch the makeup. Burning your bank-busting designer shoes or refusing to wash your hair won't make you feel better about the way you look. The key here is learning to appreciate how important your appearance is in the wider scheme of things. Think of yourself as a grand theatre production. You can use props to enhance and illustrate. You can use clever tricks to conceal and reveal parts of you. But nobody except you can write the script. No theatre critic ever said, 'Marvellous play. The script was abysmal but the set looked fantastic, and the costumes were *so* pretty!' The essence of the production is your personality. If you take it away, all you're left with is an empty theatre. The most important parts of you can't be found in your Wonderbra or beneath your mascara. What makes up the real you are your loves, hates, emotions, beliefs, humour, sexiness, confidence. And the real you is what other people care about.

17. Enjoy your body

Remembering the functionality of our body is key to improving our body image, not just in the bedroom but in every minute of every day. If we only see our bodies in terms of how they look, we'll never be satisfied. Look at the other women in the office, down the street and in your family: they don't look like stick-thin celebrities. But we don't use these women as role models. Instead we look to international supermodels and A-list movie stars. We look into the mirror and we don't resemble them so we feel ugly. We set ourselves ridiculous standards of attractiveness. So if attractiveness is the only goal we set our bodies, they will always fail.

We need to appreciate what our bodies can do for us. Use yours to the best of its ability. Look at your legs and say, 'Even though they make me feel a bit gangly, my long legs make me a great runner.' Do yoga, aerobics, walk a little faster to the bus stop, anything that teaches you what your body can do for you, rather than criticising what it looks like. It's fine to feel sexy, it's great when you feel you look good, but don't let this be the be-all and end-all. Your body serves many more purposes. We have to start appreciating this, and begin valuing our bodies in different ways.

The Rules

It's time for us to make peace with the way we look. Think of it as teamwork. If you work with your body, accepting the things you don't like and appreciating the things you do, you will feel better about it. If we constantly fight against our body, we will feel worse about ourselves. A new body rulebook needs to be written:

Rule one. Do not blame your body for every problem in life

Blaming everything on our body is the easy way out. It means we don't have to get to the root of a problem. But, inevitably, the problems will re-surface. Part of learning to accept our bodies is appreciating why we feel so lousy about them in the first place. And often we don't really hate our bottom or our skin, we hate the memories and experiences we associate with it. We hate our skin because it reminds us of bullying in the school playground, or our bottom because our first boyfriend told us that it was too big. We hold on to these things, and they cloud our judgement. By letting go of these memories, you free yourself. Ask other people what they love about your body – and listen. You aren't that kid in the playground any more, and people do not see you through your memories. Don't be the only one who can't see your body realistically. Because if you are, you're probably missing out on a great view.

Rule two. Don't treat appearance as the be-all and end-all

We must acknowledge that the way we look is only a major factor in life if we let it become so. Yes, looks can open a few doors, but so can a cracking personality. And looks will fade, body fashions change, but you will always have the ability to make people love you, laugh with you and warm to you. These are some of the most important things in life and they have nothing to do with looks. Knock your appearance down a few notches on your priority scale. We've all been bowled over by someone who isn't necessarily a supermodel, but who has a magnetic personality, and you can do just the same thing.

Rule three. Be realistic about your appearance

Remember that Body Shop campaign – three billion women in the world who don't look like supermodels and only eight who do. Body proportions to rival Barbie's are not realistic, so don't beat yourself up for not having them. Don't use impossibly beautiful supermodels as your body benchmarks. When you think about it, it is illogical to base your beauty standards on someone who has probably been airbrushed in every photo that has ever been taken of them. Don't let beauty be your goal: let health and happiness be your goal. Aim to be the happiest, healthiest 'you' that you can be. As well as improving the way you look, your confidence and self-belief will soar. Sometimes success isn't about changing the way you try to achieve your goals, it's about changing the goals you set yourself in the first place.

Stop seeing your body as the enemy. See it as a friend, an accomplice. Sometimes it will upset you. Sometimes it will make you feel bad about yourself. But, as in any other relationship, you get out of it what you put in. Learning to love your body is the best step you can take towards improving your general confidence. And the irony is that once you do that, you gain the ability to see how unimportant your appearance is in the grand scheme of things. The real world doesn't care about hips, thighs, bums and bald patches, and once you establish a healthy relationship with your own body, neither will you.

When I walked into the office I could practically hear my heart pounding. I sat down at my desk and started to shuffle papers around. Don't lose your nerve, I thought to myself as I contemplated how to do it. I noticed James looking at me from across the room.

He caught me staring at him and before I could duck under my desk and hide, he smiled and began to walk over. By this point I was so nervous that my heart felt as if it was going to explode and I thought I was going to vomit the breakfast I'd been too nervous to eat.

'Hi, Sarah,' he said in his usual suave, sexy voice. 'I heard you were shortlisted. Great news! When's the interview?'

'Er, in two weeks' time . . . Speaking of which, in, er, three and a half weeks, not two weeks, but speaking of weeks in general, I mean . . . my cousin's getting married!'

'Oh, er . . . that's nice,' he said, nervously patting his hair.

'Yeah, and I, um, well I was wondering if you're into weddings – not into them as if you collect bouquets or anything, I mean into them as in you like going to them . . . not all the time but you know . . . sometimes . . . at, er, . . . weekends.'

'Yeah, I like, um, to go to weddings sometimes.'

'Cool, 'cause I, er, I need to take a guest with me, you know how they do the invitations, "Sarah and guest", sort of like "don't bother coming alone, you need a guest to get in here!" Yeah, well, I thought if you're free in, er, three and a half weeks from now, then maybe you could be the, er, guest that Bea is referring to in the invitation?'

At this point silence fell and James just stood there looking at me in astonishment. I could feel the blood draining from my face. I'd made a complete fool of myself and he was obviously shocked that I'd asked him out. As I contemplated a way to get out of this humiliating mess, perhaps by committing hara-kiri with my plastic fountain pen, I heard him speak but didn't catch what he said. 'What?' I asked.

'I'd love to, Sarah,' he said, smiling broadly.

'Really?' I asked, unfortunately with far more surprise and relief in my voice than I'd intended.

'Of course! I've been trying to get the guts to ask you out for months.'

'You have?' Again, way too much surprise and glee in my tone.

'God, yeah! I tried to impress you with my dancing at the spring ball, which obviously didn't work, and I kept coming over with ridiculous questions about the Strazzo account just to speak to you, and you kept avoiding me, and then a few weeks ago when you saw me on the high street . . . I was sure you knew then – I mean, who buys shorts in November? It was just a lame excuse to see you.'

'But if you . . . Well, why . . . I don't get it – why didn't you just ask me out?'

'Um, well . . . you know I'm a little, er, not that confident because of my, um, looks.'

'Your looks? Are you mad? You're gorgeous!' I shrieked, getting the attention of the few remaining people in the office who hadn't noticed what was going on.

'But my hair – that day on the high street I was coming out of the hair clinic because, well, it's starting to thin at the sides here, and, er, well, I hate it, and I thought you did too.'

I couldn't believe it. All the time I'd been worrying about my bum, he'd been worrying about his hair. He had the same screwed-up world-view I did . . . I'd met my soulmate. I took him by the hand and led him to the warm golden glow of the photocopier room, where we giggled about his hair and my bum, and made plans to dance together all night long at Bea's wedding, because we were so happy to finally be together and because we loved the way we looked in each other's eyes . . .

TAKE AWAYS

In this final chapter we took stock of how far we've come and reinforced all the ideas that have come out of reading and doing the exercises in the book. It's important that you acknowledge your achievements and that you maintain them. Use this chapter to refer back to specific areas that you feel negative about – in fact, you may want to put some of the information in this chapter on cue cards to help you cope with difficult experiences you anticipate. The main thing to take away from this chapter, and the book, is that it's important to continue identifying and challenging the negative thoughts you have about your body. If you find yourself feeling anxious about your appearance because of a new experience or event, use the deep relaxation and imagery techniques (see pages 130 and 132) you have learnt. Finally, but very importantly, make a point of valuing yourself and how you look rather than putting yourself down. Liking your body image is liking the real you.

TASK 1

Dig out the task sheets you completed in the earlier chapters. Make a note of where you think you've improved and take the time to acknowledge to yourself the effort you've made in improving your body image. Also, look at the areas you still need to work on, and focus on particular difficulties by referring back to the relevant chapters and tasks until you feel you've mastered them.

TASK 2

In life we all have our rocks – wonderful friends or family members we can count on when things go wrong. It's a good idea to enlist them to help you as you work towards or try to maintain a new body image. Share with them ways that they can help you, or any anxieties you feel you need help with. Most importantly, remember that allowing yourself to look at who you are through the eyes of someone who cares about you is one of the best ways to get a clearer picture of what you look like.

TASK 3

Remember that to sustain a better body image it's not enough to close this book and forget everything you've done. Sustain your gains by making sure that you take them with you into your everyday life. Get out your diary and note down something positive that you will do for your body each day. From simple things like focusing on something you like about yourself when you look in the mirror to engaging in a sport you enjoy at weekends, include activities that feel good for you.

arlene, *Am I Thin Enough Yet?*, 1996,
rsity Press

senbaum, M. and Hirsch, J., 'Changes in
iture resulting from altered body weight',
ngland Journal of Medicine, 332(10),

Culture and Weight Consciousness, 1997,

1 Watson, J., *The Body in Everyday Life*,
ge

a, *Gender, Power and Organisation: A
perspective*, 1996, Routledge

Herman, Peter, *Breaking the Diet Habit*,
oks

and Holmes, *Other Cultures, Elder Years*,
olications

. and Schulkin, Jay (eds.), *Extreme Fear:
cial phobias*, 1999, Oxford University Press

mal models of obesity: A classification
zation', 1984, *International Journal of
–508

rri, M.G. and Kerzner, A.B., 'Do behav-
its of obesity last? A five year follow up
984, *Addictive Behaviour*, 9, 175–83

Why We Buy: The science of shopping,
Schuster

*he Skinny on Fat: Our obsession with
1999, W. H. Freeman

a, *Why Women Need Chocolate*, 1999,
olications

*e Beauty Myth: How images of beauty
women*, 1991, Vintage

Epilogue

One of my favourite literary works is Homer's epic poem *The Odyssey*. The reason that I like it so much is because it beautifully describes the idea that life is all about the journey and not really about a destination. I guess that's the way I see body image. Good body image is something you need to work at every day, making a point of addressing negative thoughts when they creep up on you, and affirming what you like about yourself. Even if there was a destination called 'perfect body image', what would really matter would be the efforts that we made to get there, and what we learnt about ourselves along the way.

We are all on a journey in life towards self-acceptance, and acceptance of our bodies is a huge part of that. As we go along, we will all be confronted with our own riddles and monsters, but what will make us healthier people is not avoiding these obstacles but facing up to them, having the confidence and the skills to learn and grow, no matter what life throws at us. That's what I have tried to do with this book — to give you some ammunition, some tools to battle your monsters with, whether they come in the shape of rude comments, the media or painful childhood memories. You see, the truth is that the riddles and monsters only really ever reside in our minds, and it's our fears and insecurities about our appearance that keep us shackled and limit the lives we allow ourselves to lead. Once we are able to free our minds of these limiting thoughts then, no doubt, our lives will follow. I hope you continue to nurture and develop your self-acceptance, and I hope the healthier body image you've attained (and will continue to build upon) will help you enjoy your journey, wherever your intended destination may be . . .

Body Shop campa
web/tbsgl/value
Cash, Thomas F.,
programme for
Harbinger Pub
Cash, Thomas F.
A handbook o
Guilford Press
Chapman, James
patients'", Da
Desmond, Sinea
January 7 200
Evans, Mary and
ical introducti
Food 24 websit
Food24/Comp
html
Forgas, Joseph
of social inte
Game, Ann and
Allen & Unv
Grogan, Sarah,
faction in m

Hesse-Biber, S
Oxford Univ
Leibel, R.L., Ro
energy expen
1995, New
621–8
Nasser, Mervat
Routledge
Nettleton, S. an
1998, Routled
Nicholson, Pau
psychological
Polivy, Janet and
1983, Basic B
Rhoads, Holmes
1995, Sage Pu
Schmidt, Louis
Shyness and so
Sclafani, A., 'An
and character
Obesity, 8, 49
Stalonas, P.M., P
ioural treatme
investigation',
Underhill, Paco,
2000, Simon &
Vogel, Shawna,
weight control
Waterhouse, Del
Waterhouse Pu
Woolf, Naomi, T
are used again

REFERENCE LIST

Voros, Sharon, 'Weight Discrimination Runs Rampant in Hiring', *Wall Street Journal, www.careerjournal.com/myc/climbing/20000905-voros.html*